# RUTH FIELDING DOWN EAST

## Or, The Hermit of Beach Plum Point

## ALICE B. EMERSON

1st WORLD
LIBRARY
Literary Society

# Ruth Fielding Down East

## Alice B. Emerson

© 1st World Library, 2009
PO Box 2211
Fairfield, IA 52556
www.1stworldlibrary.com
First Edition

LCCN: 2009923332

Softcover ISBN: 978-1-4218-8804-0
Hardcover ISBN: 978-1-4218-8903-0
eBook ISBN: 978-1-4218-8705-0

Purchase *"Ruth Fielding Down East"*
as a traditional bound book at:
www.1stWorldLibrary.com/purchase.asp?ISBN=978-1-4218-8804-0

1st World Library is a literary, educational organization
dedicated to:

- Creating a free internet library of downloadable ebooks

- Hosting writing competitions and offering book publishing
scholarships.

---

Interested in more 1st World Library books? contact:
literacy@1stworldlibrary.com
Check us out at: www.1stworldlibrary.com

# 1<sup>st</sup> World Library Literary Society

## Giving Back to the World

"If you want to work on the core problem, it's early school literacy."

**- James Barksdale, former CEO of Netscape**

"No skill is more crucial to the future of a child, or to a democratic and prosperous society, than literacy."

**- Los Angeles Times**

"Literacy... means far more than learning how to read and write... The aim is to transmit... knowledge and promote social participation."

**- UNESCO**

"Literacy is not a luxury, it is a right and a responsibility. If our world is to meet the challenges of the twenty-first century we must harness the energy and creativity of all our citizens."

**- President Bill Clinton**

"Parents should be encouraged to read to their children, and teachers should be equipped with all available techniques for teaching literacy, so the varying needs and capacities of individual kids can be taken into account."

**- Hugh Mackay**

# CONTENTS

# CHAPTER I

## THE WIND STORM

Across the now placidly flowing Lumano where it widened into almost the proportions of a lake just below the picturesque Red Mill, a bank of tempestuous clouds was shouldering into view above the sky line of the rugged and wooded hills. These slate-colored clouds, edged with pallid light, foredoomed the continuance of the peaceful summer afternoon.

Not a breath of air stirred on the near side of the river. The huge old elms shading the Red Mill and the farmhouse connected with it belonging to Mr. Jabez Potter, the miller, were like painted trees, so still were they. The brooding heat of midday, however, had presaged the coming storm, and it had been prepared for at mill and farmhouse. The tempest was due soon.

The backyard of the farmhouse—a beautiful lawn of short grass—sloped down to the river. On the bank and over the stream itself was set a summer-house of fair proportions, covered with vines—a cool and shady retreat on the very hottest day of midsummer.

A big robin redbreast had been calling his raucous weather

warning from the top of one of the trees near the house; but, with her back to the river and the coming storm, the girl in the pavilion gave little heed to this good-intentioned weather prophet.

She did raise her eyes, however, at the querulous whistle of a striped creeper that was wriggling through the intertwined branches of the trumpet-vine in search of insects. Ruth Fielding was always interested in those busy, helpful little songsters.

"You cute little thing!" she murmured, at last catching sight of the flashing bird between the stems of the old vine. "I wish I could put *you* into my scenario."

On the table at which she was sitting was a packet of type-written sheets which she had been annotating, and two fat note books. She laid down her gold-mounted fountain pen as she uttered these words, and then sighed and pushed her chair back from the table.

Then she stood up suddenly. A sound had startled her. She looked all about the summer-house—a sharp, suspicious glance. Then she tiptoed to the door and peered out.

The creeper fluttered away. The robin continued to shout his warning. Had it really been a rustling in the vines she had heard? Was there somebody lurking about the summer-house?

She stepped out and looked on both sides. It was then she saw how threatening the aspect of the clouds on the other side of the river were. The sight drove from her thoughts for the moment the strange sound she had heard. She did not take pains to look beneath the summer-house on the water side.

Alice B. Emerson

Instead, another sound assailed her ears. This time one that she could not mistake for anything but just what it was—the musical horn of Tom Cameron's automobile. Ruth turned swiftly to look up the road. A dark maroon car, long and low-hung like a racer, was coming along the road, leaving a funnel of dust behind it. There were two people in the car.

The girl beside the driver—black-haired and petite—fluttered her handkerchief in greeting when she saw Ruth standing by the summer-house. At once the latter ran across the yard, over the gentle rise, and down to the front gate of the Potter farmhouse. She ran splendidly with a free stride of untrammeled limbs, but she held one shoulder rather stiffly.

"Oh, Ruth!"

"Oh, Helen!"

The car was at the gate, and Tom brought it to a prompt stop. Helen, his twin sister, was out of it instantly and almost leaped into the bigger girl's arms.

"Oh! Oh! Oh!" sobbed Helen. "You *are* alive after all that horrible experience coming home from Europe."

"And you are alive and safe, dear Helen," responded Ruth Fielding, quite as deeply moved.

It was the first time they had met since separating in Paris a month before. And in these times of war, with peace still an uncertainty, there were many perils to fear between the port of Brest and that of New York.

Tom, in uniform and with a ribbon and medal on his breast, grinned teasingly at the two girls.

"Come, come! Break away! Only twenty seconds allowed in a clinch. Don't Helen look fine, Ruth? How's the shoulder?"

"Just a bit stiff yet," replied the girl of the Red Mill, kissing her chum again.

At this moment the first sudden swoop of the tempest arrived. The tall elms writhed as though taken with St. Vitus's dance. The hens began to screech and run to cover. Thunder muttered in the distance.

"Oh, dear me!" gasped Ruth, paling unwontedly, for she was not by nature a nervous girl. "Come right into the house, Helen. You could not get to Cheslow or back home before this storm breaks. Put your car under the shed, Tom."

She dragged her friend into the yard and up the warped flag stones to the side door of the cottage. A little old woman who had been sitting on the porch in a low rocking chair arose with difficulty, leaning on a cane.

"Oh, my back, and oh, my bones!" murmured Aunt Alvirah Boggs, who was not long out of a sick bed herself and would never again be as "spry" as she once had been. "Do come in, dearies. It is a wind storm."

Ruth stopped to help the little old woman. She continued pale, but her thought for Aunt Alvirah's comfort caused her to put aside her own fear. The trio entered the house and closed the door.

In a moment there was a sharp patter against the house. The rain had begun in big drops. The rear door was opened, and Tom, laughing and shaking the water from his cap, dashed into the living room. He wore the insignia of a captain under his dust-coat and the distinguishing marks of a very famous

Alice B. Emerson

division of the A. E. F.

"It's a buster!" he declared. "There's a paper sailing like a kite over the roof of the old mill—"

Ruth sprang up with a shriek. She ran to the back door by which Tom had just entered and tore it open.

"Oh, do shut the door, deary!" begged Aunt Alvirah. "That wind is 'nough to lift the roof."

"What *is* the matter, Ruth?" demanded Helen.

But Tom ran out after her. He saw the girl leap from the porch and run madly down the path toward the summer-house. Back on the wind came a broken word or two of explanation:

"My papers! My scenario! The best thing I ever did, Tom!"

He had almost caught up to her when she reached the little pavilion. The wind from across the river was tearing through the summer-house at a sixty-mile-an-hour speed.

"Oh! It's gone!" Ruth cried, and had Tom not caught her she would have dropped to the ground.

There was not a scrap of paper left upon the table, nor anywhere in the place. Even the two fat notebooks had disappeared, and, too, the gold-mounted pen the girl of the Red Mill had been using. All, all seemed to have been swept out of the summer-house.

## CHAPTER II

## THE MYSTERY OF IT

For half a minute Tom Cameron did not know just what to do for Ruth. Then the water spilled out of the angry clouds overhead and bade fair to drench them.

He half carried Ruth into the summer-house and let her rest upon a bench, sitting beside her with his arm tenderly supporting her shoulders. Ruth had begun to sob tempestuously.

Ruth Fielding weeping! She might have cried many times in the past, but almost always in secret. Tom, who knew her so well, had seen her in dangerous and fear-compelling situations, and she had not wept.

"What is it?" he demanded. "What have you lost?"

"My scenario! All my work gone!"

"The new story? My goodness, Ruth, it couldn't have blown away!"

"But it has!" she wailed. "Not a scrap of it left. My notebooks—my pen! Why!" and she suddenly controlled her sobs, for she was, after all, an eminently practical girl.

Alice B. Emerson

"Could that fountain pen have been carried away by the windstorm, too?"

"There goes a barrel through the air," shouted Tom. "That's heavier than a fountain pen. Say, this is some wind!"

The sound of the dashing rain now almost drowned their voices. It sprayed them through the porous shelter of the vines and latticework so that they could not sit on the bench.

Ruth huddled upon the table with Tom Cameron standing between her and the drifting mist of the storm. She looked across the rain-drenched yard to the low-roofed house. She had first seen it with a home-hungry heart when a little girl and an orphan.

How many, many strange experiences she had had since that time, which seemed so long ago! Nor had she then dreamed, as "Ruth Fielding of the Red Mill," as the first volume of this series is called, that she would lead the eventful life she had since that hour.

Under the niggard care of miserly old Jabez Potter, the miller, her great uncle, tempered by the loving kindness of Aunt Alvirah Boggs, the miller's housekeeper, Ruth's prospects had been poor indeed. But Providence moves in mysterious ways. Seemingly unexpected chances had broadened Ruth's outlook on life and given her advantages that few girls in her sphere secure.

First she was enabled to go to a famous boarding school, Briarwood Hall, with her dearest chum, Helen Cameron. There she began to make friends and widen her experience by travel. With Helen, Tom, and other young friends, Ruth had adventures, as the titles of the series of books run, at Snow Camp, at Lighthouse Point, at Silver Ranch, on Cliff

Island, at Sunrise Farm, with the Gypsies, in Moving Pictures, and Down in Dixie.

With the eleventh volume of the series Ruth and her chums, Helen Cameron and Jennie Stone, begin their life at Ardmore College. As freshmen their experiences are related in "Ruth Fielding at College; Or, The Missing Examination Papers." This volume is followed by "Ruth Fielding in the Saddle; Or, College Girls in the Land of Gold," wherein Ruth's first big scenario is produced by the Alectrion Film Corporation.

As was the fact with so many of our college boys and girls, the World War interfered most abruptly and terribly with Ruth's peaceful current of life. America went into the war and Ruth into Red Cross work almost simultaneously.

In "Ruth Fielding in the Red Cross; Or, Doing Her Bit for Uncle Sam," the Girl of the Red Mill gained a very practical experience in the work of the great peace organization which does so much to smooth the ravages of war. Then, in "Ruth Fielding at the War Front; Or, The Hunt for the Lost Soldier," the Red Cross worker was thrown into the very heart of the tremendous struggle, and in northern France achieved a name for courage that her college mates greatly envied.

Wounded and nerve-racked because of her experiences, Ruth was sent home, only to meet, as related in the fifteenth volume of the series, "Ruth Fielding Homeward Bound; Or, A Red Cross Worker's Ocean Perils," an experience which seemed at first to be disastrous. In the end, however, the girl reached the Red Mill in a physical and mental state which made any undue excitement almost a tragedy for her.

The mysterious disappearance of the moving picture scenario, which had been on her heart and mind for months and which she had finally brought, she believed, to a successful termination, actually shocked Ruth Fielding. She could not control herself for the moment.

Against Tom Cameron's uniformed shoulder she sobbed frankly. His arm stole around her.

"Don't take on so, Ruthie," he urged. "Of course we'll find it all. Wait till this rain stops—"

"It never blew away, Tom," she said.

"Why, of course it did!"

"No. The sheets of typewritten manuscript were fastened together with a big brass clip. Had they been lose and the wind taken them, we should have seen at least some of them flying about. And the notebooks!"

"And the pen?" murmured Tom, seeing the catastrophe now as she did. "Why, Ruthie! Could somebody have taken them all?"

"Somebody must!"

"But who?" demanded the young fellow. "You have no enemies."

"Not here, I hope," she sighed. "I left them all behind."

He chuckled, although he was by no means unappreciative of the seriousness of her loss. "Surely that German aviator who dropped the bomb on you hasn't followed you here."

"Don't talk foolishly, Tom!" exclaimed the girl, getting back some of her usual good sense. "Of course, I have no enemy.

But a thief is every honest person's enemy."

"Granted. But where is the thief around the Red Mill?"

"I do not know."

"Can it be possible that your uncle or Ben saw the things here and rescued them just before the storm burst?"

"We will ask," she said, with a sigh. "But I can imagine no reason for either Uncle Jabez or Ben to come down here to the shore of the river. Oh, Tom! it is letting up."

"Good! I'll look around first of all. If there has been a skulker near—"

"Now, don't be rash," she cried.

"We're not behind the German lines now, Fraulein Mina von Brenner," and he laughed as he went out of the summer-house.

He did not smile when he was searching under the house and beating the brush clumps near by. He realized that this loss was a very serious matter for Ruth.

She was now independent of Uncle Jabez, but her income was partly derived from her moving picture royalties. During her war activities she had been unable to do much work, and Tom knew that Ruth had spent of her own means a great deal in the Red Cross work.

Ruth had refused to tell her friends the first thing about this new story for the screen. She believed it to be the very best thing she had ever originated, and she said she wished to surprise them all.

Alice B. Emerson

He even knew that all her notes and "before-the-finish" writing was in the notebooks that had now gone with the completed manuscript. It looked more than mysterious. It was suspicious.

Tom looked all around the summer-house. Of course, after this hard downpour it was impossible to mark any footsteps. Nor, indeed, did the raider need to leave such a trail in getting to and departing from the little vine-covered pavilion. The sward was heavy all about it save on the river side.

The young man found not a trace. Nor did he see a piece of paper anywhere. He was confident that Ruth's papers and notebooks and pen had been removed by some human agency. And it could not have been a friend who had done this thing.

# CHAPTER III

## THE DERELICT

"Didn't you find anything, Tom?" Ruth Fielding asked, as Helen's twin re-entered the summer-house.

His long automobile coat glistened with wet and his face was wind-blown. Tom Cameron's face, too, looked much older than it had—well, say a year before. He, like Ruth herself, had been through much in the war zone calculated to make him more sedate and serious than a college undergraduate is supposed to be.

"I did not see even a piece of paper blowing about," he told her.

"But before we came down from the house you said you saw a paper blow over the roof like a kite."

"That was an outspread newspaper. It was not a sheet of your manuscript."

"Then it all must have been stolen!" she cried.

"At least, human agency must have removed the things you left on this table," he said.

Alice B. Emerson

"Oh, Tom!"

"Now, now, Ruth! It's tough, I know—"

But she recovered a measure of her composure almost immediately. Unnerved as she had first been by the disaster, she realized that to give way to her trouble would not do the least bit of good.

"An ordinary thief," Tom suggested after a moment, "would not consider your notes and the play of much value."

"I suppose not," she replied.

"If they are stolen it must be by somebody who under-stands—or thinks he does—the value of the work. Somebody who thinks he can sell a moving picture scenario."

"Oh, Tom!"

"A gold mounted fountain pen would attract any petty thief," he went on to say. "But surely the itching fingers of such a person would not be tempted by that scenario."

"Then, which breed of thief stole my scenario, Tom?" she demanded. "You are no detective. Your deductions suggest two thieves."

"Humph! So they do. Maybe they run in pairs. But I can't really imagine two light-fingered people around the Red Mill at once. Seen any tramps lately?"

"We seldom see the usual tramp around here," said Ruth, shaking her head. "We are too far off the railroad line. And the Cheslow constables keep them moving if they land *there*."

"Could anybody have done it for a joke?" asked Tom suddenly.

"If they have," Ruth said, wiping her eyes, "it is the least like a joke of anything that ever happened to me. Why, Tom! I couldn't lay out that scenario again, and think of all the details, and get it just so, in a year!"

"Oh, Ruth!"

"I mean it! And even my notes are gone. Oh, dear! I'd never have the heart to write that scenario again. I don't know that I shall ever write another, anyway. I'm discouraged," sobbed the girl suddenly.

"Oh, Ruth! don't give way like this," he urged, with rather a boyish fear of a girl's tears.

"I've given way already," she choked. "I just feel that I'll never be able to put that scenario into shape again. And I'd written Mr. Hammond so enthusiastically about it."

"Oh! Then he knows all about it!" said Tom. "That is more than any of us do. You wouldn't tell us a thing."

"And I didn't tell him. He doesn't know the subject, or the title, or anything about it. I tell you, Tom, I had *such* a good idea—"

"And you've got the idea yet, haven't you? Cheer up! Of course you can do it over."

"Suppose," demanded Ruth quickly, "this thief that has got my manuscript should offer it to some producer? Why! if I tried to rewrite it and bring it out, I might be accused of plagiarizing my own work."

"Jimminy!"

"I wouldn't dare," said Ruth, shaking her head. "As long as I do not know what has become of the scenario and my notes, I will not dare use the idea at all. It is dreadful!"

The rain was now falling less torrentially. The tempest was passing. Soon there was even a rift in the clouds in the northwest where a patch of blue sky shone through "big enough to make a Scotchman a pair of breeches," as Aunt Alvirah would say.

"We'd better go up to the house," sighed Ruth.

"I'll go right around to the neighbors and see if anybody has noticed a stranger in the vicinity," Tom suggested.

"There's Ben! Do you suppose he has seen anybody?"

A lanky young man, his clothing gray with flour dust, came from the back door of the mill and hastened under the dripping trees to reach the porch of the farmhouse. He stood there, smiling broadly at them, as Ruth and Tom hurriedly crossed the yard.

"Good day, Mr. Tom," said Ben, the miller's helper. Then he saw Ruth's troubled countenance. "Wha—what's the matter, Ruthie?"

"Ben, I've lost something."

"Bless us an' save us, no!"

"Yes, I have. Something very valuable. It's been stolen."

"You don't mean it!"

"But I do! Some manuscript out of the summer-house yonder."

"And her gold-mounted fountain pen," added Tom. "That would tempt somebody."

"My goodness!"

Ben could express his simple wonderment in a variety of phrases. But he seemed unable to go beyond these explosive expressions.

"Ben, wake up!" exclaimed Ruth. "Have you any idea who would have taken it?"

"That gold pen, Ruthie? Why—why—A thief!"

"Old man," said Tom with suppressed disgust, "you're a wonder. How did you guess it?"

"Hush, Tom," Ruth said. Then: "Now, Ben, just think. Who has been around here to-day? Any stranger, I mean."

"Why—I dunno," said the mill hand, puckering his brows.

"Think!" she commanded again.

"Why—why—old Jep Parloe drove up for a grinding."

"He's not a stranger."

"Oh, yes he is, Ruthie. Me nor Mr. Potter ain't seen him before for nigh three months. Your uncle up and said to him, 'Why, you're a stranger, Mr. Parloe.'"

"I mean," said Ruth, with patience, "anybody whom you

Alice B. Emerson

have never seen before—or anybody whom you might suspect would steal."

"Well," drawled Ben stubbornly, "your uncle, Ruthie, says old Jep ain't any too honest."

"I know all about that," Ruth said. "But Parloe did not leave his team and go down to the summer-house, did he?"

"Oh, no!"

"Did you see anybody go down that way?"

"Don't believe I did—savin' you yourself, Ruthie."

"I left a manuscript and my pen on the table there. I ran out to meet Tom and Helen when they came."

"I seen you," said Ben.

"Then it was just about that time that somebody sneaked into that summer-house and stole those things."

"I didn't see anybody snuck in there," declared Ben, with more confidence than good English.

"Say!" ejaculated Tom, impatiently, "haven't you seen any tramp, or straggler, or Gypsy—or anybody like that?"

"Hi gorry!" suddenly said Ben, "I do remember. There was a man along here this morning—a preacher, or something like that. Had a black frock coat on and wore his hair long and sort o' wavy. He was shabby enough to be a tramp, that's a fact. But he was a real knowledgeable feller—he was that. Stood at the mill door and recited po'try for us."

"Poetry!" exclaimed Tom.

"To you and Uncle Jabez?" asked Ruth.

"Uh-huh. All about 'to be or not to be a bean—that is the question.' And something about his having suffered from the slung shots and bow arrers of outrageous fortune—whatever that might be. I guess he got it all out of the Scriptures. Your uncle said he was bugs; but I reckoned he was a preacher."

"Jimminy!" muttered Tom. "A derelict actor, I bet. Sounds like a Shakespearean ham."

"Goodness!" said Ruth. "Between the two of you boys I get a very strange idea of this person."

"Where did he go, Ben?" Tom asked.

"I didn't watch him. He only hung around a little while. I think he axed your uncle for some money, or mebbe something to eat. You see, he didn't know Mr. Potter."

"Not if he struck him for a hand-out," muttered the slangy Tom.

"Oh, Ben! don't you know whether he went toward Cheslow —or where?" cried Ruth.

"Does it look probable to you," Tom asked, "that a derelict actor—Oh, Jimminy! Of course! *He* would be just the person to see the value of that play script at a glance!"

"Oh, Tom!"

"Have you no idea where he went, Ben?" Tom again demanded of the puzzled mill hand.

"No, Mister Tom. I didn't watch him."

"I'll get out the car at once and hunt all about for him," Tom said quickly. "You go in to Helen and Aunt Alvirah, Ruth. You'll be sick if you let this get the best of you. I'll find that miserable thief of a ham actor—if he's to be found." He added this last under his breath as he ran for the shed where he had sheltered his automobile.

# CHAPTER IV

## THE CRYING NEED

Tom Cameron chased about the neighborhood for more than two hours in his fast car hunting the trail of the man who he had decided must be a wandering theatrical performer. Of course, this was a "long shot," Tom said; but the trampish individual of whom Ben had told was much more likely to be an actor than a preacher.

Tom, however, was able to find no trace of the fellow until he got to the outskirts of Cheslow, the nearest town. Here he found a man who had seen a long-haired fellow in a shabby frock coat and black hat riding toward the railroad station beside one of the farmers who lived beyond the Red Mill. This was following the tempest which had burst over the neighborhood at mid-afternoon.

Trailing this information farther, Tom learned that the shabby man had been seen about the railroad yards. Mr. Curtis, the railroad station master, had observed him. But suddenly the tramp had disappeared. Whether he had hopped Number 10, bound north, or Number 43, bound south, both of which trains had pulled out of Cheslow within the hour, nobody could be sure.

Alice B. Emerson

Tom returned to the Red Mill at dusk, forced to report utter failure.

"If that bum actor stole your play, Ruth, he's got clear way with it," Tom said bluntly. "I'm awfully sorry—"

"Does that help?" demanded his sister snappishly, as though it were somewhat Tom's fault. "You go home, Tom. I'm going to stay with Ruthie to-night," and she followed her chum into the bedroom to which she had fled at Tom's announcement of failure.

"Jimminy!" murmured Tom to the old miller who was still at the supper table. "And we aren't even sure that that fellow did steal the scenario."

"Humph!" rejoined Uncle Jabez. "You'll find, if you live to be old enough, young feller, that women folks is kittle cattle. No knowing how they'll take anything. That pen cost five dollars, I allow; but them papers only had writing on 'em, and it does seem to me that what you have writ once you ought to be able to write again. That's the woman of it. She don't say a thing about that pen, Ruthie don't."

However, Tom Cameron saw farther into the mystery than Uncle Jabez appeared to. And after a day or two, with Ruth still "moping about like a moulting hen," as the miller expressed it, the young officer felt that he must do something to change the atmosphere of the Red Mill farmhouse.

"Our morale has gone stale, girls," he declared to his sister and Ruth. "Worrying never did any good yet."

"That's a true word, Sonny," said Aunt Alvirah, from her chair. "'Care killed the cat.' my old mother always said, and she had ten children to bring up and a drunken husband who was a trial. He warn't my father. He was her second, an' she took him, I guess, 'cause he was ornamental. He was a sign painter when he worked. But he mostly advertised King Alcohol by painting his nose red.

"We children sartain sure despised that man. But mother was faithful to her vows, and she made quite a decent member of the community of that man before she left off. And, le's see! We was talkin' about cats, warn't we?"

"You were, Aunty dear," said Ruth, laughing for the first time in several days.

"Hurrah!" said Tom, plunging head-first into his idea. "That's just what I wanted to hear."

"What?" demanded Helen.

"I have wanted to hear Ruth laugh. And we all need to laugh. Why, we are becoming a trio of old fogies!"

"Speak for yourself, Master Tom," pouted his sister.

"I do. And for you. And certainly Ruth is about as cheerful as a funeral mute. What we all need is some fun."

"Oh, Tom, I don't feel at all like 'funning,'" sighed Ruth.

"You be right, Sonny," interjected Aunt Alvirah, who sometimes forgot that Tom, as well as the girls, was grown up. She rose from her chair with her usual, "Oh, my back! and oh, my bones! You young folks should be dancing and frolicking—"

"But the war, Auntie!" murmured Ruth.

"You'll neither make peace nor mar it by worriting. No, no, my pretty! And 'tis a bad thing when young folks grow old before their time."

"You're always saying that, Aunt Alvirah," Ruth complained. "But how can one be jolly if one does not feel jolly?"

"My goodness!" cried Tom, "you were notoriously the jolliest girl in that French hospital. Didn't the *poilus* call you the jolly American? And listen to Grandmother Grunt now!"

"I suppose it is so," sighed Ruth. "But I must have used up all my fund of cheerfulness for those poor *blesses*. It does seem as though the font of my jollity had quite dried up."

"I wish Heavy Stone were here," said Helen suddenly. "*She'd* make us laugh."

"She and her French colonel are spooning down there at Lighthouse Point," scoffed Ruth—and not at all as Ruth Fielding was wont to speak.

"Say!" Tom interjected, "I bet Heavy is funny even when she is in love."

"*That's* a reputation!" murmured Ruth.

"They are not at Lighthouse Point. The Stones did not go there this summer, I understand," Helen observed.

"I am sorry for Jennie and Colonel Marchand if they are at the Stones' city house at this time of the year," the girl of the Red Mill said.

"Bully!" cried Tom, with sudden animation. "That's just what we will do!"

"What will we do, crazy?" demanded his twin.

"We'll get Jennie Stone and Henri Marchand—he's a good sport, too, as I very well know—and we'll all go for a motor trip. Jimminy Christmas! that will be just the thing, Sis. We'll go all over New England, if you like. We'll go Down East and introduce Colonel Marchand to some of our hard-headed and tight-fisted Yankees that have done their share towards injecting America into the war. We will—"

"Oh!" cried Ruth, breaking in with some small enthusiasm, "let's go to Beach Plum Point."

"Where is that?" asked Helen.

"It is down in Maine. Beyond Portland. And Mr. Hammond and his company are there making my 'Seaside Idyl.'"

"Oh, bully!" cried Helen, repeating one of her brother's favorite phrases, and now quite as excited over the idea as he. "I do so love to act in movies. Is there a part in that 'Idyl' story for me?"

"I cannot promise that," Ruth said. "It would be up to the director. I wasn't taking much interest in this particular picture. I wrote the scenario, you know, before I went to France. I have been giving all my thought to—

"Oh, dear! If we could only find my lost story!"

"Come on!" interrupted Tom. "Let's not talk about that. Will you write to Jennie Stone?"

"I will. At once," his sister declared.

"Do. I'll take it to the post office and send it special delivery.

Tell her to wire her answer, and let it be 'yes.' We'll take both cars. Father won't mind."

"Oh, *but*!" cried Helen. "How about a chaperon?"

"Oh, shucks! I wish you'd marry some nice fellow, Sis, so that we'd always have a chaperon on tap and handy."

She made a little face at him. "I am going to be old-maid aunt to your many children, Tommy-boy. I am sure you will have a full quiver. We will have to look for a chaperon."

"Aunt Kate!" exclaimed Ruth. "Heavy's Aunt Kate. She is just what Helen declares she wants to be—an old-maid aunt."

"And a lovely lady," cried Helen.

"Sure. Ask her. Beg her," agreed Tom. "Tell her it is the crying need. We have positively got to have some fun."

"Well, I suppose we may as well," Ruth sighed, in agreement.

"Yes. We have always pampered the boy," declared Helen, her eyes twinkling. "I know just what I'll wear, Ruthie."

"Oh, we've clothes enough," admitted the girl of the Red Mill rather listlessly.

"Shucks!" said Tom again. "Never mind the fashions. Get that letter written, Sis."

So it was agreed. Helen wrote, the letter was sent. With Jennie Stone's usual impulsiveness she accepted for herself and "*mon Henri*" and Aunt Kate, promising to be at Cheslow within three days, and all within the limits of a ten-word telegram!

Alice B. Emerson

# CHAPTER V

## OFF AT LAST

"The ancients," stated Jennie Stone solemnly, "burned incense upon any and all occasions—red letter days, labor days, celebrating Columbus Day and the morning after, I presume. But we moderns burn gasoline. And, phew! I believe I should prefer the stale smoke of incense in the unventilated pyramids of Egypt to this odor of gas. O-o-o-o, Tommy, do let us get started!"

"You've started already—in your usual way," he laughed.

This was at Cheslow Station on the arrival of the afternoon up train that had brought Miss Stone, her Aunt Kate, and the smiling Colonel Henri Marchand to join the automobile touring party which Jennie soon dubbed "the later Pilgrims."

"And that big machine looks much as the *Mayflower* must have looked steering across Cape Cod Bay on that special occasion we read of in sacred and profane history, hung about with four-poster beds and whatnots. In our neighborhood," the plump girl added, "there is enough decrepit furniture declared to have been brought over on the *Mayflower* to have made a cargo for the *Leviathan*."

"Oh, *ma chere!* you do but stretch the point, eh?" demanded the handsome Henri Marchand, amazed.

"I assure you—"

"Don't, Heavy," advised Helen. "You will only go farther and do worse. In my mind there has always been a suspicion that the *Mayflower* was sent over here by some shipped knocked-down furniture factory. Miles Standish and Priscilla Mullins and John Alden must have hung on by their eyebrows."

"Their eyebrows—*ma foi!*" gasped Marchand.

"Say, old man," said Tom, laughing, "if you listen to these crazy college girls you will have a fine idea of our historical monuments, and so forth. Take everything with a grain of salt—do."

"*Oui, Monsieur!* But I must have a little pepper, too. I am 'strong,' as you Americans say, for plentiful seasoning."

"Isn't he cute?" demanded Jenny Stone. "He takes to American slang like a bird to the air."

"Poetry barred!" declared Helen.

"Say," Tom remarked aside to the colonel, "you've got all the pep necessary, sure enough, in Jennie."

"She is one dear!" sighed the Frenchman.

"And she just said you were a bird. You'll have a regular zoo about you yet. Come on. Let's see if we can get this baggage aboard the good ship. It does look a good deal of an ark, doesn't it?"

Alice B. Emerson

Although Ruth and Aunt Kate had not joined in this repartee, the girl of the Red Mill, as well as their lovely chaperon, enjoyed the fun immensely. Ruth had revived in spirits on meeting her friends. Jennie had flown to her arms at the first greeting, and hugged the girl of the Red Mill with due regard to the mending shoulder.

"My dear! My dear!" she had cried. "I *dream* of you lying all so pale and bloody under that window-sill stone. And what I hear of your and Tom's experiences coming over—"

"But worse has happened to me since I arrived home," Ruth said woefully.

"No? Impossible!"

"Yes. I have had an irreparable loss," sighed Ruth. "I'll tell you about it later."

But for the most part the greetings of the two parties was made up as Tom said of "Ohs and Ahs."

"Take it from me," the naughty Tom declared to Marchand, "two girls separated for over-night can find more to tell each other about the next morning than we could think of if we should meet at the Resurrection!"

The two Cameron cars stood in the station yard, and as the other waiting cars, taxicabs and "flivvers" departed, "the sacred odor of gasoline," which Jennie had remarked upon, was soon dissipated.

The big touring car was expertly packed with baggage, and had a big hamper on either running-board as well. There was room remaining, however, for the ladies if they would sit there. But as Tom was to drive the big car he insisted that

Ruth sit with him in the front seat for company. As for his racing car, he had turned that over to Marchand. It, too, was well laden; but at the start Jennie squeezed in beside her colonel, and the maroon speeder was at once whisperingly dubbed by the others "the honeymoon car."

"Poor children!" said Aunt Kate in private to the two other girls. "They cannot marry until the war is over. *That* my brother is firm upon, although he thinks well of Colonel Henri. And who could help liking him? He is a most lovable boy."

"'Boy!'" repeated Ruth. "And he is one of the most famous spies France has produced in this war! And a great actor!"

"But we believe he is not acting when he tells us he loves Jennie," Aunt Kate said.

"Surely not!" cried Helen.

"He is the soul of honor," Ruth declared. "I trust him as I do —well, Tom. I never had a brother."

"I've always shared Tom with you," pouted Helen.

"So you have, dear," admitted Ruth. "But a girl who has had no really-truly brother really has missed something. Perhaps good, perhaps bad. But, at least, if you have brothers you understand men better."

"Listen to the wisdom of the owl!" scoffed Helen. "Why, Tommy is only a girl turned inside out. A girl keeps all her best and softest attributes to the fore, while a boy thinks it is more manly to show a prickly surface—like the burr of a chestnut."

Alice B. Emerson

"Listen to them!" exclaimed Aunt Kate, with laughter. "All the wise sayings of the ancient world must be crammed under those pretty caps you wear, along with your hair."

"That is what we get at college," said Helen seriously. "Dear old Ardmore! Ruth! won't you be glad to get back to the grind again?"

"I—don't—know," said her chum slowly. "We have seen so much greater things than college. It's going to be rather tame, isn't it?"

But this conversation was all before they were distributed into their seats and had started. Colonel Marchand was an excellent driver, and he soon understood clearly the mechanism of the smaller car. Tom gave him the directions for the first few miles and they pulled out of the yard with Mr. Curtis, the station master, and his lame daughter, who now acted as telegraph operator, waving the party good-bye.

They would not go by the way of the Red Mill, for that would take them out of the way they had chosen. The inn they had in mind to stop at on this first night was a long four hours' ride.

"Eastward, Ho!" shouted Tom. "This is to be a voyage of discovery, but don't discover any punctures or blow-outs this evening."

Then he glanced at Ruth's rather serious face beside him and muttered to himself:

"And we want to discover principally the smile that Ruth Fielding seems to have permanently lost!"

# CHAPTER VI

## "THE NEVERGETOVERS"

After crossing the Cheslow Hills and the Lumano by the Long Bridge about twenty miles below the Red Mill, the touring party debouched upon one of the very best State roads. They left much of the dust from which they had first suffered behind them, and Tom could now lead the way with the big car without smothering the occupants of the honeymoon car in the rear.

The highway wound along a pretty ridge for some miles, with farms dotting the landscape and lush meadows or fruit-growing farms dipping to the edge of the distant river.

"Ah," sighed Henri Marchand. "Like *la belle* France before the war. Such peace and quietude we knew, too. Fortunate you are, my friends, that *le Boche* has not trampled these fields into bloody mire."

This comment he made when they halted the cars at a certain overlook to view the landscape. But they could not stop often. Their first objective inn was still a long way ahead.

They did not, however, reach the inn, which was a resort well known to motorists. Five miles away Tom noticed that

Alice B. Emerson

the car was acting strangely.

"What is it, Tom?" demanded Ruth quickly.

"Steering gear, I am afraid. Something is loose."

It did not take him long to make an examination, and in the meantime the second car came alongside.

"It might hold out until we get to the hotel ahead; but I think we had better stop before that time if we can," was Tom's comment. "I do not want the thing to break and send us flying over a stone wall or up a tree."

"But you can fix it, Tom?" questioned Ruth.

"Sure! But it will take half an hour or more."

After that they ran along slowly and presently came in sight of a place called the Drovers' Tavern.

"Not a very inviting place, but I guess it will do," was Ruth's announcement after they had looked the inn over.

The girls and Aunt Kate alighted at the steps while the young men wheeled the cars around to the sheds.

The housekeeper, who immediately announced herself as Susan Timmins, was fussily determined to see that all was as it should be in the ladies' chambers.

"I can't trust this gal I got to do the upstairs work," she declared, saying it through her nose and with emphasis. "Just as sure as kin be, if ye go for to help a poor relation you air always sorry for it."

She led the way up the main flight of stairs as she talked.

"This here gal will give me the nevergitovers, I know! She's my own sister's child that married a good-for-nothing and is jest like her father."

"Bella! You Bella! Turn on the light in these rooms. Is the pitchers filled? And the beds turned down? If I find a speck of dust on this furniture I'll nigh 'bout have the nevergitovers! That gal will drive me to my grave, she will. Bella!"

Bella appeared—a rather good looking child of fourteen or so, slim as a lath and with hungry eyes. She was dark—almost Gypsy-like. She stared at Ruth, Helen and Jennie with all the amazement of the usual yokel. But it was their dress, not themselves, Ruth saw, engaged Bella's interest.

"When you ladies want any help, you call for Bella," announced Miss Susan Timmins. "And if she don't come running, you let me know, and I'll give her her nevergitovers, now I tell ye!"

"No wonder this hotel is called 'Drovers' Tavern,'" said Jennie Stone. "That woman certainly is a driver—a slave driver."

Ruth, meanwhile, was trying to make a friend of Bella.

"What is your name, my dear?" she asked the lathlike girl.

"You heard it," was the ungracious reply.

"Oh! Yes. 'Bella.' But your other name?"

"Arabella Montague Fitzmaurice Pike. My father is Montague Fitzmaurice."

She said it proudly, with a lift of her tousled head and a straightening of her thin shoulders.

"Oh!" fairly gasped Ruth Fielding. "It—it sounds quite impressive, I must say. I guess you think a good deal of your father?"

"Aunt Suse don't," said the girl ungraciously. "My mother's dead. And pa is resting this season. So I hafter stay here with Aunt Suse. I hate it!"

"Your father is—er—what is his business?" Ruth asked.

"He's one of the profession."

"A doctor?"

"Lands, no! He's a heavy."

"A *what*?"

"A heavy lead—and a good one. But these moving pictures knock out all the really good people. There are no chances now for him to play Shakespearean roles—"

"Your father is an actor!" cried Ruth.

"Of course. Montague Fitzmaurice. Surely you have heard the name?" said the lathlike girl, tossing her head.

"Why—why—of course!" declared Ruth warmly. It was true. She had heard the name. Bella had just pronounced it!

"Then you know what kind of an actor my pa is," said the proud child. "He did not have a very good season last winter. He rehearsed with four companies and was only out three weeks altogether. And one of the managers did not pay at all."

"That is too bad."

"Yes. It's tough," admitted Bella. "But I liked it."

"You liked it when he was so unsuccessful?" repeated Ruth.

"Pa wasn't unsuccessful. He never is. He can play any part," declared the girl proudly. "But the plays were punk. He says there are no good plays written nowadays. That is why so many companies fail."

"But you said you liked it?"

"In New York," explained Bella. "While he was rehearsing pa could get credit at Mother Grubson's boarding house on West Forty-fourth Street. I helped her around the house. She said I was worth my keep. But Aunt Suse says I don't earn my salt here."

"I am sure you do your best, Bella," Ruth observed.

"No, I don't. Nor you wouldn't if you worked for Aunt Suse. She says I'll give her her nevergitovers—an' I hope I do!" with which final observation she ran to unlace Aunt Kate's shoes.

"Poor little thing," said Ruth to Helen. "She is worse off than an orphan. Her Aunt Susan is worse than Uncle Jabez ever was to me. And she has no Aunt Alvirah to help her to bear it. We ought to do something for her."

"There! You've begun. Every waif and stray on our journey must be aided, I suppose," pouted Helen, half exasperated.

But Tom was glad to see that Ruth had found a new interest. Bella waited on the supper table, was snapped at by Miss Timmins, and driven from pillar to post by that crotchety individual.

"Jimminy Christmas!" remarked Tom, "that Timmins woman must be a reincarnation of one of the ancient Egyptians who was overseer in the brickyard where Moses learned his trade. If they were all like her, no wonder the Israelites went on a strike and marched out of Egypt."

They were all very careful, however, not to let Miss Susan Timmins hear their comments. She had the true dictatorial spirit of the old-fashioned New England school teacher. The guests of Drovers' Tavern were treated by her much as she might have treated a class in the little red schoolhouse up the road had she presided there.

She drove the guests to their chambers by the method of turning off the electric light in the general sitting room at a quarter past ten. Each room was furnished with a bayberry candle, and she announced that the electricity all over the house would be switched off at eleven o'clock.

"That is late enough for any decent body to be up," she announced in her decisive manner. "That's when I go to bed myself. I couldn't do so in peace if I knew folks was burning them electric lights to all hours. 'Tain't safe in a thunder storm.

"Why, when we first got 'em, Jed Parraday from Wachuset come to town to do his buyin' and stayed all night with us. He'd never seed a 'lectric bulb before, and he didn't know how to blow it out. And he couldn't sleep in a room with a light.

"So, what does the tarnal old fool do but unhook the cord so't the bulb could be carried as far as the winder. And he hung it outside, shut the winder down on it, drawed the shade and went to bed in the dark.

"Elnathan Spear, the constable, seen the light a-shining outside the winder in the middle of the night and he thought 'twas burglars. He *dreams* of burglars, Elnathan does. But he ain't never caught none yet.

"On that occasion, howsomever, he was sure he'd got a whole gang of 'em, and he waked up the whole hotel trying to find out what was going on. I charged Parraday ha'f a dollar for burning extry 'lectricity, and he got so mad he ain't stopped at the hotel since.

"He'd give one the nevergitovers, that man would!" she concluded.

# CHAPTER VII

## MOVIE STUNTS

Jennie Stone slept in Ruth's bed that night because, having been parted since they were both in France, they had a great deal to say to each other—thus proving true one of Tom Cameron's statements regarding women.

Jennie was just as sympathetic—and as sleepy—as she could be and she "oh, dear, me'd" and yawned alternately all through the tale of the lost scenario and notebooks, appreciating fully how Ruth felt about it, but unable to smother the expression of her desire for sleep.

"Maybe we ought not to have come on this automobile trip," said Jennie. "If the thief just did it to be mean and is somebody who lives around the Red Mill, perhaps you might have discovered something by mingling with the neighbors."

"Oh! Tom did all that," sighed Ruth. "And without avail. He searched the neighborhood thoroughly, although he is confident that a tramp carried it off. And that seems reasonable. I am almost sure, Heavy, that my scenario will appear under the trademark of some other producing manager than Mr. Hammond."

"Oh! How mean!"

"Well, a thief is almost the meanest person there is in the world, don't you think so? Except a backbiter. And anybody mean enough to steal my scenario must be mean enough to try to make use of it."

"Oh, dear! Ow-oo-ooo! Scuse me, Ruth. Yes, I guess you are right. But can't you stop the production of the picture?"

"How can I do that?"

"I don't—ow-oo!—know. Scuse me, dear."

"Most pictures are made in secret, anyway. The public knows nothing about them until the producer is ready to make their release."

"I—ow-oo!—I see," yawned Jennie.

"Even the picture play magazines do not announce them until the first runs. Then, sometimes, there is a synopsis of the story published. But it will be too late, then. Especially when I have no notes of my work, nor any witnesses. I told no living soul about the scenario—what it was about, or—"

"Sh-sh-sh—"

"Why, Heavy!" murmured the scandalized Ruth.

"Sh-sh-sh—whoo!" breathed the plump girl, with complete abandon.

"My goodness!" exclaimed Ruth, tempted to shake her, "if you snore like that when you are married, Henri will have to sleep at the other end of the house."

Alice B. Emerson

But this was completely lost on the tired Jennie Stone, who continued to breathe heavily until Ruth herself fell asleep. It seemed as though the latter had only closed her eyes when the sun shining into her face awoke the girl of the Red Mill. The shades of the east window had been left up, and it was sunrise.

Plenty of farm noises outside the Drovers' Tavern, as well as a stir in the kitchen, assured Ruth that there were early risers here. Jennie, rolled in more than her share of the bedclothes, continued to breathe as heavily as she had the night before.

But suddenly Ruth was aware that there was somebody besides herself awake in the room. She sat up abruptly in bed and reached to seize Jennie's plump shoulder. Ruth had to confess she was much excited, if not frightened.

Then, before she touched the still sleeping Jennie Stone, Ruth saw the intruder. The door from the anteroom was ajar. A steaming agateware can of water stood on the floor just inside this door. Before the bureau which boasted a rather large mirror for a country hotel bedroom, pivoted the thin figure of Arabella Montague Fitzmaurice Pike!

From the neatly arranged outer clothing of the two girls supposedly asleep in the big four-poster, Bella had selected a skirt of Ruth's and a shirt-waist of Jennie's, arraying herself in both of these borrowed garments. She was now putting the finishing touch to her costume by setting Ruth's cap on top of her black, fly-away mop of hair.

Turning about and about before the glass, Bella was so much engaged in admiring herself that she forgot the hot water she was supposed to carry to the various rooms. Nor did she see Ruth sitting up in bed looking at her in dawning amusement. Nor did she, as she pirouetted there, hear her Nemesis outside in the hall.

The door suddenly creaked farther open. The grim face of Miss Susan Timmins appeared at the aperture.

"Oh!" gasped Ruth Fielding aloud.

Bella turned to glance in startled surprise at the girl in bed. And at that moment Miss Timmins bore down upon the child like a shrike on a chippy-bird.

"Ow-ouch!" shrieked Bella.

"Oh, don't!" begged Ruth.

"What is it? Goodness! *Fire!*" cried Jennie Stone, who, when awakened suddenly, always remembered the dormitory fire at Briarwood Hall.

"You little pest! I'll larrup ye good! I'll give ye your nevergitovers!" sputtered the hotel housekeeper.

But the affrighted Bella wriggled away from her aunt's bony grasp. She dodged Miss Timmins about the marble-topped table, retreated behind the hair-cloth sofa, and finally made a headlong dash for the door, while Jennie continued to shriek for the fire department.

Ruth leaped out of bed. In her silk pajamas and slippers, and without any wrap, she hurried to reach, and try to separate, the struggling couple near the door.

Miss Timmins delivered several hearty slaps upon Bella's face and ears. The child shrieked. She got away again and plunged into the can of hot water.

Alice B. Emerson

Over this went, flooding the rag-carpet for yards around.

"Fire! Fire!" Jennie continued to shriek.

Helen dashed in from the next room, dressed quite as lightly as Ruth, and just in time to see the can spilled.

"Oh! Water! Water!"

"Drat that young one!" barked Miss Timmins, ignoring the flood and everything else save her niece—even the conventions.

She dashed after Bella. The latter had disappeared into the hall through the anteroom.

"Oh, the poor child!" cried sympathetic Ruth, and followed in the wake of the angry housekeeper.

"Fire! Fire!" moaned Jennie Stone.

"Cat's foot!" snapped Helen Cameron. "It's water—and it is flooding the whole room."

She ran to set the can upright—after the water was all out of it. Without thinking of her costume, Ruth Fielding ran to avert Bella's punishment if she could. She knew the aunt was beside herself with rage, and Ruth feared that the woman would, indeed, give Bella her "nevergetovers."

The corridor of the hotel was long, running from front to rear of the main building. The window at the rear end of it overlooked the roof of the back kitchen. This window was open, and when Ruth reached the corridor Bella was going head-first through the open window, like a circus clown diving through a hoop.

She had discarded Jennie's shirt-waist between the bedroom and the window. But Ruth's skirt still flapped about the child's thin shanks.

Miss Timmins, breathing threatenings and slaughter, raced down the hall in pursuit. Ruth followed, begging for quarter for the terrified child.

But the housekeeper went through the open window after Bella, although in a more conventional manner, paying no heed to Ruth's plea. The frightened girl, however, escaped her aunt's clutch by slipping off the borrowed skirt and descending the trumpet-vine trellis by the kitchen door.

"Do let her go, Miss Timmins!" begged Ruth, as the panting woman, carrying Ruth's skirt, returned to the window where the girl of the Red Mill stood. "She is scared to death. She was doing no harm."

"I'll thank you to mind your own business, Miss," snapped Miss Timmins hotly. "I declare! A girl growed like you running 'round in men's overalls—or, what be them things you got on?"

At this criticism Ruth Fielding fled, taking the skirt and Jennie's shirt-waist with her. But Aunt Kate was aroused now and the four women of the automobile party swiftly slipped into their negligees and appeared in the hall again, to meet Tom and Colonel Marchand who came from their room only partly dressed.

The critical Miss Timmins had darted downstairs, evidently in pursuit of her unfortunate niece. The guests crowded to the back window.

"Where did she go?" demanded Tom, who had heard some

Alice B. Emerson

explanation of the early morning excitement. "Is she running away?"

"What a child!" gasped Aunt Kate.

"My waist!" moaned Jennie.

"Look at Ruth's skirt!" exclaimed Helen.

"I do not care for the skirt," the girl of the Red Mill declared. "It is Bella."

"Her aunt will about give her those 'nevergetovers' she spoke of," chuckled Tom.

"*Ma foi!* look you there," exclaimed Colonel Marchand, pointing through the window that overlooked the rear premises of the hotel.

At top speed Miss Timmins was crossing the yard toward the big hay barn. Bella had taken refuge in that structure, and the housekeeper's evident intention was to harry her out. The woman grasped a clothes-stick with which she proposed to castigate her niece.

"The cruel thing!" exclaimed Helen, the waters of her sympathy rising for Bella Pike now.

"There's the poor kid!" said Tom.

Bella appeared at an open door far up in the peak of the haymow. The hay was packed solidly under the roof; but there was an air space left at either end.

"She has put herself into the so-tight corner—no?" suggested the young Frenchman.

"You've said it!" agreed Tom. "Why! it's regular movie stunts. She's come up the ladders to the top of the mow. If auntie follows her, I don't see that the kid can do anything but jump!"

"Tom! Never!" cried Ruth.

"He is fooling," said Jennie.

"Tell me how she can dodge that woman, then," demanded Tom.

"Ah!" murmured Henri Marchand. "She have arrive'."

Miss Timmins appeared at the door behind Bella. The spectators heard the girl's shriek. The housekeeper struck at her with the clothes stick. And then—

"Talk about movie stunts!" shouted Tom Cameron, for the frightened Bella leaped like a cat upon the haymow door and swung outward with nothing more stable than air between her and the ground, more than thirty feet below!

Alice B. Emerson

# CHAPTER VIII

## THE AUCTION BLOCK

Helen Cameron and Jennie Stone shrieked in unison when Miss Susan Timmins' niece cast herself out of the haymow upon the plank door and swung as far as the door would go upon its creaking hinges. Ruth seized Tom's wrist in a nervous grip, but did not utter a word. Aunt Kate turned away and covered her eyes with her hands that she might not see the reckless child fall—if she did fall.

"Name of a name!" murmured Henri Marchand. "*Au secours!* Come, Tom, *mon ami*—to the rescue!"

He turned and ran lightly along the hall and down the stairs. But Tom went through the window, almost as precipitately as had Bella Pike herself, and so over the roof of the kitchen ell and down the trumpet-vine trellis.

Tom was in the yard and running to the barn before Marchand got out of the kitchen. Several other people, early as the hour was, appeared running toward the rear premises of Drovers' Tavern.

"See that crazy young one!" some woman shrieked. "I know she'll kill herself yet."

"Stop that!" commanded Tom, looking up and shaking a threatening hand at Miss Timmins.

For in her rage the woman was trying to strike her niece with the stick, as Bella clung to the door.

"Mind your own business, young man!" snapped the virago. "And go back and put the rest of your clothes on. You ain't decent."

Tom was scarcely embarrassed by this verbal attack. The case was too serious for that. Miss Timmins struck at the girl again, and only missed the screaming Bella by an inch or so.

Helen and Jennie screamed in unison, and Ruth herself had difficulty in keeping her lips closed. The cruel rage of the hotel housekeeper made her quite unfit to manage such a child as Bella, and Ruth determined to interfere in Bella's behalf at the proper time.

"I wish she would pitch out of that door herself!" cried Helen recklessly.

Tom had run into the barn and was climbing the ladders as rapidly as possible to the highest loft. Scolding and striking at her victim, Miss Susan Timmins continued to act like the mad woman she was. And Bella, made desperate at last by fear, reached for the curling edges of the shingles on the eaves above her head.

"Don't do that, child!" shrieked Jennie Stone.

But Bella scrambled up off the swinging door and pulled herself by her thin arms on to the roof of the barn. There she was completely out of her aunt's reach.

"Oh, the plucky little sprite!" cried Helen, in delight.

"But—but she can't get down again," murmured Aunt Kate. "There is no scuttle in that roof."

"Tom will find a way," declared Ruth Fielding with confidence.

"And my Henri," put in Jennie. "That horrid old creature!"

"She should be punished for this," agreed Ruth. "I wonder where the child's father is."

"Didn't you find out last night?" Helen asked.

"Only that he is 'resting'."

"Some poor, miserable loafer, is he?" demanded Aunt Kate, with acrimony.

"No. It seems that he is an actor," Ruth explained. "He is out of work."

"But he can't think anything of his daughter to see her treated like this," concluded Aunt Kate.

"She is very proud of him. His professional name is Montague Fitzmaurice."

"Some name!" murmured Jennie.

"Their family name is Pike," said Ruth, still seriously. "I do not think the man can know how this aunt treats little Bella. There's Tom!"

The young captain appeared behind the enraged housekeeper

at the open door of the loft. One glance told him what Bella had done. He placed a firm hand on Miss Timmins' shoulder.

"If you had made that girl fall you would go to jail," Tom said sternly. "You may go, yet. I will try to put you there. And in any case you shall not have the management of the child any longer. Go back to the house!"

For once the housekeeper was awed. Especially when Henri Marchand, too, appeared in the loft.

"Madame will return to the house. We shall see what can be done for the child. *Gare!*"

Perhaps the woman was a little frightened at last by what she had done—or what she might have done. At least, she descended the ladders to the ground floor without argument.

The two young men planned swiftly how to rescue the sobbing child. But when Tom first spoke to Bella, proposing to help her down, she looked over the edge of the roof at him and shook her head.

"No! I ain't coming down," she announced emphatically. "Aunt Suse will near about skin me alive."

"She shall not touch you," Tom promised.

"She'll give me my nevergitovers, just as she says. You can't stay here and watch her."

"But we'll find a way to keep her from beating you when we are gone," Tom promised. "Don't you fear her at all."

"I don't care where you put me, Aunt Suse will find me out. She'll send Elnathan Spear after me."

Alice B. Emerson

"I don't know who Spear is—"

"He's the constable," sobbed Bella.

"Well, he sha'n't spear you," declared Tom. "Come on, kid. Don't be scared, and we'll get you down all right."

He found the clothes-stick Miss Timmins had abandoned and used it for a brace. With a rope tied to the handle of the plank door and drawn taut, it was held half open. Tom then climbed out upon and straddled the door and raised his arms to receive the girl when she lowered herself over the eaves.

She was light enough—little more than skin and bone, Tom declared—and the latter lowered her without much effort into Henri's arms.

When the three girls and Aunt Kate at the tavern window saw this safely accomplished they hurried back to their rooms to dress.

"Something must be done for that poor child," Ruth Fielding said with decision.

"Are you going to adopt her?" Helen asked.

"And send her to Briarwood?" put in Jennie.

"That might be the very best thing that could happen to her," Ruth rejoined soberly. "She has lived at times in a theatrical boarding house and has likewise traveled with her father when he was with a more or less prosperous company.

"These experiences have made her, after a fashion, grown-up in her ways and words. But in most things she is just as ignorant as she can be. Her future is not the most important thing just now. It is her present."

Helen heard the last word from the other room where she was dressing, and she cried:

"That's it, Ruthie. Give her a present and tell her to run away from her aunt. She's a spiteful old thing!"

"You do not mean that!" exclaimed her chum. "You are only lazy and hate responsibility of any kind. We must do something practical for Bella Pike."

"How easily she says 'we'," Helen scoffed.

"I mean it. I could not sleep to-night if I knew this child was in her aunt's control."

A knock on the door interrupted the discussion. Ruth, who was quite dressed now, responded. A lout of a boy, who evidently worked about the stables, stood grinning at the door.

"Miz Timmins says you folks kin all get out. She won't have you served no breakfast. She don't want none of you here."

"My goodness!" wailed Jennie. "Dispossessed—and without breakfast!"

"Where is the proprietor of this hotel, boy?" Ruth asked.

"You mean Mr. Drovers? He ain't here. Gone to Boston. But that wouldn't make no dif'rence. Suse Timmins is boss."

"Oh, me! Oh, my!" groaned Jennie, to whom the prospect was tragic. Jennie's appetite was never-failing.

Alice B. Emerson

The boy slouched away just as Tom and Henri Marchand appeared with Bella between them.

"You poor, dear child!" cried Ruth, running along the hall to meet them.

Bella struggled to escape from the boys. But Tom and Colonel Marchand held her by either hand.

"Easy, young one!" advised Captain Cameron.

"I never meant to do no harm, Miss!" cried Bella. "I—I just wanted to see how I'd look in them clothes. I never do have anything decent to wear."

"Why, my dear, don't mind about that," said Ruth, taking the lathlike girl in her arms. "If you had asked us we would have let you try on the things, I am sure."

"Aunt Suse would near 'bout give me my nevergitovers—and she will yet!"

"No she won't," Ruth reassured her. "Don't be afraid of your aunt any longer."

"That is what I tell her," Tom said warmly.

"Say! You won't put me in no home, will you?" asked Bella, with sudden anxiety.

"A 'home'?" repeated Ruth, puzzled.

"She means a charitable institution, poor dear," said Aunt Kate.

"That's it, Missus," Bella said. "I knew a girl that was out of one of them homes. She worked for Mrs. Grubson. She said all the girls wore brown denim uniforms and had their hair slicked back and wasn't allowed even to whisper at table or after they got to bed at night."

"Nothing like that shall happen to you," Ruth declared.

"Where is your father, Bella?" Tom asked.

"I don't know. Last I saw of him he came through here with a medicine show. I didn't tell Aunt Suse, but I ran away at night and went to Broxton to see him. But he said business was poor. He got paid so much a bottle commission on the sales of Chief Henry Red-dog's Bitters. He didn't think the show would keep going much longer."

"Oh!"

"You know, they didn't know he was Montague Fitzmaurice, the great Shakespearean actor. Pa often takes such jobs. He ain't lazy like Aunt Suse says. Why, once he took a job as a ballyhoo at a show on the Bowery in Coney Island. But his voice ain't never been what it was since."

"Do you expect him to return here for you?" Ruth asked, while the other listeners exchanged glances and with difficulty kept their faces straight.

"Oh, yes, Miss. Just as soon as he is in funds. Or he'll send for me. He always does. He knows I hate it here."

"Does he know how your aunt treats you?" Aunt Kate interrupted.

"N—not exactly," stammered Bella. "I haven't told him all. I don't want to bother him. It—it ain't always so bad."

"I tell you it's got to stop!" Tom said, with warmth.

"Of course she shall not remain in this woman's care any longer," Aunt Kate agreed.

"But we must not take Bella away from this locality," Ruth observed. "When her father comes back for her she must be here—somewhere."

"Oh, lady!" exclaimed Bella. "Send me to New York to Mrs. Grubson's. I bet she'd keep me till pa opens somewhere in a good show."

But Ruth shook her head. She had her doubts about the wisdom of the child's being in such a place as Mrs. Grubson's boarding house, no matter how kindly disposed that woman might be.

"Bella should stay near here," Ruth said firmly, "as long as we cannot communicate with Mr. Pike at once."

"Let's write a notice for one of the theatrical papers," suggested Helen eagerly. "You know—'Montague Fitzmaurice please answer.' All the actors do it."

"But pa don't always have the money to buy the papers," said Bella, taking the suggestion quite seriously.

"At least, if Bella is in this neighborhood he will know where to find her," went on Ruth. "Is there nobody you know here, child, whom you would like to stay with till your father returns?"

Bella's face instantly brightened. Her black eyes flashed.

"Oh, I'd like to stay at the minister's," she said.

"At the minister's?" repeated Ruth. "Why, if he would take you that would be fine. Who is he?"

"The Reverend Driggs," said Bella.

"Do you suppose the clergyman would take the child?" murmured Aunt Kate.

"Why do you want to go to live with the minister?" asked Tom with curiosity.

"'Cause he reads the Bible so beautifully," declared Bella. "Why! it sounds just like pa reading a play. The Reverend Driggs is an educated man like pa. But he's got an awful raft of young ones."

"A poor minister," said Aunt Kate briskly. "I am afraid that would not suit."

"If the Driggs family is already a large one," began Ruth doubtfully, when Bella declared:

"Miz Driggs had two pairs of twins, and one ever so many times. There's a raft of 'em."

Helen and Jennie burst out laughing at this statement and the others were amused. But to Ruth Fielding this was a serious matter. The placing of Bella Pike in a pleasant home until her father could be communicated with, or until he appeared on the scene ready and able to care for the child, was even more serious than the matter of going without breakfast, although Jennie Stone said "No!" to this.

"We'd better set up an auction block before the door of the hotel and auction her off to the highest bidder, hadn't we?" suggested Helen, who had been rummaging in her bag.

"Here, Bella! If you want a shirt-waist to take the place of that calico blouse you have on, here is one. One of mine. And I guarantee it will fit you better than Heavy's did. She wears an extra size."

"I don't either," flashed the plump girl, as the boys retreated from the room. "I may not be a perfect thirty-six—"

"Is there any doubt of it?" cried Helen, the tease.

"Well!"

"Never mind," Ruth said. "Jennie is going to be thinner."

"And it seems she will begin to diet this very morning," Aunt Kate put in.

"Ow-wow!" moaned Jennie at this reminder that they had been refused breakfast.

Captain Tom, however, had handled too many serious situations in France to be browbeaten by a termagant like Miss Susan Timmins. He went down to the kitchen, ordered a good breakfast for all of his party, and threatened to have recourse to the law if the meal was not well and properly served.

"For you keep a public tavern," he told the sputtering Miss Timmins, "and you cannot refuse to serve travelers who are willing and able to pay. We are on a pleasure trip, and I assure you, Madam, it will be a pleasure to get you into court for any cause."

On coming back to the front of the house he found two of the neighbors just entering. One proved to be the local doctor's wife and the other was a kindly looking farmer.

"I knowed that girl warn't being treated right, right along," said the man. "And I told Mirandy that I was going to put a stop to it."

"It is a disgrace," said the doctor's wife, "that we should have allowed it to go on so long. I will take the child myself—"

"And so'll Mirandy," declared the farmer.

"It is an auction," whispered Helen, overhearing this from the top of the stairs.

The party of guests came down with their bags now, bringing Bella in their midst—and in the new shirt-waist.

"Let her choose which of these kind people she will stay with," Tom advised. "And," he added, in a low voice to Ruth, "we will pay for her support until we can find her father."

"Like fun you will, young feller!" snorted the farmer, overhearing Tom.

"I could not hear of such a thing," said the doctor's wife.

"I'd like to know what you people think you're doing?" demanded Miss Timmins, popping out at them suddenly.

"Now, Suse Timmins, we're a-goin' to do what we neighbors ought to have done long ago. We're goin' to take this gal—"

"You start anything like that—taking that young one away from her lawful guardeen—an' I'll get Elnathan Spear after you in a hurry, now I tell ye. I'll give you your nevergitovers!"

Alice B. Emerson

"If Nate Spear comes to my house, I'll ask him to pay me for that corn he bought off'n me as long ago as last fall," chuckled the farmer. "Just because you're own cousin to Nate don't put *all* the law an' the gospel on your side, Suse Timmins. I'll take good care of this girl."

"And so will I, if Bella wants to live with me," said the doctor's wife.

"Mirandy will be glad to have her."

"And she'd be company for me," rejoined the other neighbor. "I haven't any children."

"Bella must choose for herself," said Ruth kindly.

"I guess I'll go with Mr. Perkins," said the actor's daughter. "Miz Holmes is real nice; but Doctor Holmes gives awful tastin' medicine. I might be sick there and have to take some of it. So I'll go to Miz Perkins. She has a doctor from Maybridge and he gives candy-covered pellets. I ate some once. Besides, Miz Perkins is lame and can't get around so spry, and I can do more for her."

"Now listen to that!" exclaimed the farmer. "Ain't she a noticing child?"

"Well, Mrs. Perkins will be good to her, no doubt," agreed the doctor's wife.

"I'd like to know what you fresh city folks butted into this thing for!" demanded Miss Timmins. "If there's any law in the land—"

"*You'll* get it!" promised Tom Cameron.

"Go get anything you own that you want to take with you, Bella," Ruth advised the shrinking child.

With another fearful glance at her aunt, Bella ran upstairs.

Miss Timmins might have started after her, but Tom planted himself before that door. The lout of a boy began bringing in the breakfast for the automobile party. Ruth talked privately with the doctor's wife and Mr. Perkins, and forced some money on the woman to be expended for a very necessary outfit of clothing for Bella.

Miss Timmins finally flounced back into the kitchen where they heard her venting her anger and chagrin on the kitchen help. Bella returned bearing an ancient extension bag crammed full of odds and ends. She kissed Ruth and shook hands with the rest of the company before departing with Mr. Perkins.

The doctor's wife promised to write to Ruth as soon as anything was heard of Mr. Pike, and the automobile party turned their attention to ham and eggs, stewed potatoes, and griddle cakes.

"Only," said Jennie, sepulchrally, "I hope the viands are not poisoned. That Miss Timmins would certainly like to give us all our 'nevergetovers'."

# CHAPTER IX

## A DISMAYING DISCOVERY

"'The Later Pilgrims' are well out of that trouble," announced Helen, when the cars were underway, the honeymoon car ahead and the other members of the party packed into the bigger automobile.

"And I hope," she added, "that Ruth will find no more waifs and strays."

"Don't be knocking Ruthie all the time," said Tom, glancing back over his shoulder. "She's all right."

"And you keep your eyes straight ahead, young man," advised Aunt Kate, "or you will have this heavy car in the ditch."

"Watch out for Henri and Heavy, too," advised Helen. "They do not quite know what they are about and you may run them down. There! See his horizon-blue sleeve steal about her? He's got only one hand left to steer with. Talk about a perfect thirty-six! It's lucky Henri's arm is phenomenally long, or he could never surround *that* baby!"

"I declare, Helen," laughed Ruth. "I believe you are covetous."

"Well, Henri is an awfully nice fellow—for a Frenchman."

"And you are the damsel who declared you proposed to remain an old maid forever and ever and the year after."

"I can be an old maid and still like the boys, can't I? All the more, in fact. I sha'n't have to be true to just one man, which, I believe, would be tedious."

"You should live in that part of New York called Greenwich Village and wear a Russian blouse and your hair bobbed. Those are the kind of bon mots those people throw off in conversation. Light and airy persiflage, it is called," said Tom from the front seat.

"What do you know about such people, Tommy?" demanded his sister.

"There were some co-eds of that breed I met at Cambridge. They were exponents of the 'new freedom,' whatever that is. Bolshevism, I guess. Freedom from both law and morals."

"Those are not the kind of girls who are helping in France," said Ruth soberly.

"You said it!" agreed Tom. "That sort are so busy riding hobbies over here that they have no interest in what is going on in Europe unless it may be in Russia. Well, thank heaven, there are comparatively few nuts compared with us sane folks."

Such thoughts as these, however, did not occupy their minds for long. Just as Tom had declared, they were out for fun, and the fun could be found almost anywhere by these blithe young folk.

Alice B. Emerson

Ruth's face actually changed as they journeyed on. She was both "pink and pretty," Helen declared, before they camped at the wayside for luncheon.

The hampers on the big car were crammed with all the necessities of food and service for several meals. There were, too, twin alcohol lamps, a coffee boiler and a teapot.

Altogether they were making a very satisfactory meal and were having a jolly time at the edge of a piece of wood when a big, black wood-ant dropped down Jennie Stone's back.

At first they did not know what the matter was with her. Her mouth was full, the food in that state of mastication that she could not immediately swallow it.

"Ow! Ow! Ow!" choked the plump girl, trying to get both hands at once down the neck of her shirt-waist.

"What *is* the matter, Heavy?" gasped Helen.

"Jennie, dear!" murmured Ruth. "Don't!"

"*Ma chere!*" gasped Henri Marchand. "Is she ill?"

"Jennie, behave yourself!" cried her aunt.

"I saw a toad swallow a hornet once," Tom declared. "She acts just the same way."

"As the hornet?" demanded his sister, beginning to giggle.

"As the toad," answered Tom, gravely.

But Henri had got to his feet and now reached the wriggling girl. "Let me try to help!" he cried.

"If you even begin wiggling that way, Colonel Marchand," declared Helen, "you will be in danger of arrest. There is a law against *that* dance."

"Ow! Ow! Ow!" burst out Jennie once more, actually in danger of choking.

"What *is* it?" Ruth demanded, likewise reaching the writhing girl.

"Oh, he bit me!" finally exploded Jennie.

Ruth guessed what must be the trouble then, and she forced Jennie's hands out of the neck of her waist and ran her hand down the plump girl's back. Between them they killed the ant, for Ruth finally recovered a part of the unfortunate creature.

"But just think," consoled Helen, "how much more awful it would have been if you had swallowed him, Heavy, instead of his wriggling down your spinal column."

"Oh, don't! I can feel him wriggling now," sighed Jennie.

"That can be nothing more than his ghost," said Tom soberly, "for Ruth retrieved at least half of the ant's bodily presence."

"You'll give us all the fidgets if you keep on wriggling, Jennie," declared Aunt Kate.

"Well, I don't want to sit on the grass in a woodsy place again while we are on this journey," sighed Jennie. "Ugh! I always did hate creepy things."

"Including spiders, snakes, beetles and babies, I suppose?" laughed Helen. "Come on now. Let us clear up the wreck.

Where do we camp to-night, Tommy?"

"No more camping, I pray!" squealed Jennie. "I am no Gypsy."

"The hotel at Hampton is recommended as the real thing. They have a horse show every year at Hampton, you know. It is in the midst of a summer colony of wealthy people. It is the real thing," Tom repeated.

They made a pleasant and long run that afternoon and arrived at the Hampton hotel in good season to dress for dinner. Jennie and her aunt met some people they knew, and naturally Jennie's fiance and her friends were warmly welcomed by the gay little colony.

Men at the pleasure resorts were very scarce that year, and here were two perfectly good dancers. So it was very late when the automobile party got away from the dance at the Casino.

They were late the next morning in starting on the road to Boston. Besides, there was thunder early, and Helen, having heard it rumbling, quoted:

"Thunder in the morning,
Sailors take warning!"

and rolled over for another nap.

Ruth, however, at last had to get up. She was no "lie-abed" in any case, and in her present nervous state she had to be up and doing.

"But it's going to ra-a-ain!" whined Jennie Stone when Ruth went into her room.

"You're neither sugar nor salt," said Ruth.

"Henri says I'm as sweet as sugar," yawned Jennie.

"He is not responsible for what he says about you," said her aunt briskly. "When I think of what that really nice young man is taking on his shoulders when he marries you—"

"But, Auntie!" cried Jennie, "he's not going to try to carry me pickaback, you know."

"Just the same, it is wrong for us to encourage him to become responsible for you, Jennie," said her aunt. "He really should be warned."

"Oh!" gasped the plump girl. "Let anybody dare try to get between me and my Henri—"

"Nobody can—no fear—when you are sitting with him in the front seat of that roadster of Tom's," said Ruth. "You fill every atom of space, Heavy."

She went to the window and looked out again. Heavy rolled out of bed—a good deal like a barrel, her aunt said tartly.

"What is it doing outside?" yawned the plump girl.

"Well, it's not raining. And it is a long run to Boston. We should be on our way now. The road through the hills is winding. There will be no time to stop for a Gypsy picnic."

"Thank goodness for that!" grumbled Jennie, sitting on the floor, schoolgirl fashion, to draw on her stockings. "I'll eat enough at breakfast hereafter to keep me alive until we reach a hotel, if you folks insist on inviting wood ants and other savage creatures of the forest to our luncheon table."

Alice B. Emerson

When the party finally gathered for breakfast in the hotel dining room on this morning, it was disgracefully late. Tom had been over both cars and pronounced them fit. He had ordered the tanks filled with gasoline and had tipped one of the garage men liberally to see that this was properly done.

Afterward Captain Tom declared he would never trust a garage workman again.

"The only way to get a thing done well is to do it yourself—and a tip never bought any special service yet," declared the angry Tom. "It is merely a form of highway robbery."

But this was afterward. The party started off from Hampton in high fettle and with a childlike trust in the honesty of a garage attendant.

There were banks of clouds shrouding the horizon both to the west and north—the two directions from which thunder showers usually rise in this part of New England in which they were traveling. And yet the shower held off.

It was some time past noon before the thunder began to mutter again. The automobile party was then in the hilly country. Heretofore farms had been plentiful, although hamlets were few and far between.

"If it rains," said Ruth cheerfully, "of course we can take refuge in some farmhouse."

"Ho, for adventure among the savage natives!" cried Helen.

"I hope we shall meet nobody quite as savage as Miss Susan Timmins," was Aunt Kate's comment.

They ran into a deep cut between two wooded hills and there

was not a house in sight. Indeed, they had not passed a farmstead on the road for the last five miles. Over the top of the wooded crest to the north curled a slate colored storm cloud, its upper edge trembling with livid lightnings. The veriest tyro of a weather prophet could see that a storm was about to break. But nobody had foretold the sudden stopping of the honeymoon car in the lead!

"What is the matter with you?" cried Helen, standing up in the tonneau of the big car, when Tom pulled up suddenly to keep from running the maroon roadster down. "Don't you see it is going to rain? We want to get somewhere."

"I guess we have got somewhere," responded Jennie Stone. "As far as we are concerned, this seems to be our stopping place. The old car won't go."

Tom jumped out and hurried forward to join Henri in an examination of the car's mechanism.

"What happened, Colonel?" he asked the Frenchman, worriedly.

"I have no idea, *mon ami*," responded Marchand. "This is a puzzle, eh?"

"First of all, let's put up the tops. That rain is already beating the woods on the summit of the hill."

The two young men hurried to do this, first sheltering Jennie and then together dragging the heavy top over the big car, covering the baggage and passengers. Helen and Ruth could fasten the curtains, and soon the women of the party were snug enough. The drivers, however, had to get into rain garments and begin the work of hunting the trouble with the roadster.

Alice B. Emerson

The thunder grew louder and louder. Flashes of lightning streaked across the sky overhead. The electric explosions were soon so frequent and furious that the girls cowered together in real terror. Jennie had slipped out of the small car and crowded in with her chums and Aunt Kate.

"I don't care!" she wailed, "Henri and Tom are bound to take that car all to pieces to find what has happened."

But they did not have to go as far as that. In fact, before the rain really began to fall in earnest, Tom made the tragic discovery. There was scarcely a drop of gasoline in the tank of the small machine. Tom hurried back to the big car. He glanced at the dial of the gasoline tank. There was not enough of the fluid to take them a mile! And the emergency tank was turned on!

It was at this point that he stated his opinion of the trustworthiness of garage workmen.

# CHAPTER X

## A WILD AFTERNOON

This was a serious situation. Five miles behind the automobile party was the nearest dwelling on this road, and Tom
was sure that the nearest gasoline sign was all of five miles
further back!

Ahead lay more or less mystery. As the rain began to drum
upon the roofs of the two cars, harder and harder and faster
and faster, Tom got out the road map and tried to figure out
their location. Ridgeton was ahead somewhere—not nearer
than six miles, he was sure. And the map showed no gas sign
this side of Ridgeton.

Of course there might be some wayside dwelling only a short
distance ahead at which enough gasoline could be secured to
drive the smaller car to Ridgeton for a proper supply for both
machines. But if all the gasoline was drained from the tank
of the big car into that of the roadster, the latter would be
scarcely able to travel another mile. And without being sure
that such a supply of gas could be found within that distance,
why separate the two cars?

This was the sensible way Tom put it to Henri; and it was
finally decided that Tom should start out on foot with an

empty can and hunt for gasoline, while Colonel Marchand remained with the girls and Aunt Kate.

When the two young men ran back through the pouring rain to the big car and announced this decision, they had to shout to make the girls hear. The turmoil of the rain and thunder was terrific.

"I really wish you'd wait, Tom, till the tempest is over," Ruth anxiously said. "Suppose something happened to you on the road?"

"Suppose something happened to *us* here in the auto?" shrieked Helen.

"But Henri Marchand will be with you," said her brother, preparing to depart. "And if I delay we may not reach Boston to-night."

"Oh!" gasped Jennie. "Do please find some gas, Tom. I'd be scared to death to stay out here in these woods."

"One of the autos may bite her," scoffed Helen, ready to scorn her own fears when her friend was even more fearful. "These cars are the wildest thing in these woods, I warrant."

"Of course you must do what you think is best, Tom," said Ruth, gravely. "I hope you will not have to go far."

"No matter how long I am gone, Ruth, don't be alarmed," he told her. "You know, nothing serious ever happens to me."

"Oh, no!" cried his sister. "Of course not! Only you get carried away on a Zeppelin, or are captured by the Germans and Ruth has to go to your rescue. We know all about how immune you are from trouble, young man."

"Thanks be! there are no Boches here in peaceful New England," exclaimed Jennie, after Tom had started off with the gasoline can. "Oh!"

A sharp clap of thunder seemingly just overhead followed the flash that had made the plump girl shriek. The explosion reverberated between the hills in slowly passing cadence.

Jennie finally removed her fingers from her ears with a groan. Aunt Kate had covered her eyes. With Helen they cowered together in the tonneau. Ruth had been sitting beside Tom in the front seat when the cars were stalled, and now Henri Marchand was her companion.

"I heard something then, Colonel," Ruth said in a low tone, when the salvo of thunder was passed.

"You are fortunate, Mademoiselle," he returned. "Me, I am deafened complete'."

"I heard a cry."

"Not from Captain Cameron?"

"It was not his voice. Listen!" said the girl of the Red Mill, in some excitement.

Despite the driving rain she put her head out beyond the curtain and listened. Her face was sheltered from the beating rain. It would have taken her breath had she faced it. Again the lightning flashed and the thunder crashed on its trail.

Ruth did not draw in her head. She wore her raincoat and a rubber cap, and on her feet heavy shoes. The storm did not frighten her. She might be anxious for Tom's safety, but the ordinary chances of such a disturbance of the elements as

Alice B. Emerson

this never bothered Ruth Fielding at all.

As the rolling of thunder died away in the distance again, the splashing sound of the rain seemed to grow lighter, too; or Ruth's hearing became attuned to the sounds about her.

There it was again! A human cry! Or was it? It came from up the hillside to the north of the road on which the automobiles were stalled.

Was there somebody up there in the wet woods—some human creature lost in the storm?

For a third time Ruth heard the wailing, long-drawn cry. Henri had his hands full soothing Jennie. Helen and Aunt Kate were clinging together in the depths of the tonneau. Possibly their eyes were covered against the glare of the lightning.

Ruth slipped out under the curtain on the leeward side. The rain swept down the hillside in solid platoons that marched one after another from northwest to southeast. Dashing against the southern hillside, these marching columns dissolved in torrents that Ruth could hear roaring down from the tree-tops and rushing in miniature floods through the forest.

The road was all awash. The cars stood almost hub-deep in a yellow, foaming flood. The roadside ditches were not deep here, and the sudden freshet was badly guttering the highway.

Sheltered at first by the top of the big car, Ruth strained her ears again to catch that cry which had come down the wind from the thickly wooded hillside.

There it was! A high, piercing scream, as though the one who uttered it was in great fear or agony. Nor did the cry seem to be far away.

Ruth went around to the other side of the automobile. The rain was letting up—or seemed to be. She crossed to the higher ground and pushed through the fringe of bushes that bordered the road.

Already her feet and ankles were saturated, for she had waded through water more than a foot in depth. Here on the steep hillside the flowing water followed the beds of small rivulets which carried it away on either side of her.

The thick branches of the trees made an almost impervious umbrella above her head. She could see up the hill through the drifting mist for a long distance. The aisles between the rows of trees seemed filled with a sort of pallid light.

Across the line of her vision and through one of these aisles passed a figure—whether that of an animal or the stooping body of a human being Ruth Fielding could not at first be sure.

She had no fear of there being any savage creature in this wood. At least there could be nothing here that would attack her in broad daylight. In a lull in the echoing thunder she cried aloud:

"Hoo-hoo! Hoo-hoo! Where are you?"

She was sure her voice drove some distance up the hillside against the wind. She saw the flitting figure again, and with a desire to make sure of its identity, Ruth started in pursuit.

Had Tom been present the girl of the Red Mill would have

Alice B. Emerson

called his attention to the mystery and left it to him to decide whether to investigate or not. But Ruth was quite an independent person when she was alone; and under the circumstances, with Henri Marchand so busy comforting Jennie, Ruth did not consider for a moment calling the Frenchman to advise with her.

As for Helen and Aunt Kate, they were quite overcome by their fears. Ruth was not really afraid of thunder and lightning, as many people are. She had long since learned that "thunder does not bite, and the bolt of lightning that hits you, you will never see!"

Heavy as the going was, and interfering with her progress through her wet garments did, Ruth ran up the hill underneath the dripping trees. She saw the flitting, shadowy figure once more. Again she called as loudly as she could shout:

"Wait! Wait! I won't hurt you."

Whoever or whatever it was, the figure did not stay. It flitted on about two hundred yards ahead of the pursuing girl.

At times it disappeared altogether; but Ruth kept on up the hill and her quarry always reappeared. She was quite positive this was the creature that had shrieked, for the mournful cry was not repeated after she caught sight of the figure.

"It is somebody who has been frightened by the storm," she thought. "Or it is a lost child. This is a wild hillside, and one might easily be lost up here."

Then she called again. She thought the strange figure turned and hesitated. Then, of a sudden, it darted into a clump of brush. When Ruth came panting to the spot she could see no trace of the creature, or the path which it had followed.

But directly before Ruth was an opening in the hillside—the mouth of a deep ravine which had not been visible from the road below.

Down this ravine ran a noisy torrent which had cut itself a wider and deeper bed since the cloudburst on the heights. Small trees, brush, and rocks had been uprooted by the force of the stream, but its current was now receding. One might walk along the edge of the brook into this hillside fastness.

Determined to solve the mystery of the strange creature's disappearance, and quite convinced that it was a lost child or woman, Ruth Fielding ventured through the brush clump and passed along the ragged bank of the tumbling brook.

Suddenly, in the muddy ground at her feet, the girl spied a shoe. It was a black oxford of good quality, and it had been, of course, wrenched from the foot of the person she pursued. This girl, or woman, must be running from Ruth in fear.

Ruth picked up the shoe. It was for a small foot, but might belong to either a girl of fourteen or so or to a small woman. She could see the print of the other shoe—yes! and there was the impress of the stockinged foot in the mud.

"Whoever she may be," thought Ruth Fielding, "she is so frightened that she abandoned this shoe. Poor thing! What can be the matter with her?"

Ruth shouted again, and yet again. She went on up the side of the turbulent brook, staring all about for the hiding place of her quarry.

The rain ceased entirely and abruptly. But the whole forest was a-drip. Far up through the trees she saw a sudden lightening of the sky. The clouds were breaking.

Alice B. Emerson

But the smoke of the torrential downpour still rose from the saturated earth. When Ruth jarred a bush in passing a perfect deluge fell from the trembling leaves. The girl began to feel that she had come far enough in what appeared to be a wild-goose chase.

Then suddenly, quite amazingly, she was halted. She plunged around a sharp turn in the ravine, trying to step on the dryer places, and found herself confronted by a man standing under the shelter of a wide-armed spruce.

"Oh!" gasped Ruth, starting back.

He was a heavy-set, bewhiskered man with gleaming eyes and rather a grim look. Worst of all, he carried a gun with the lock sheltered under his arm-pit from the rain.

At Ruth's appearance he seemed startled, too, and he advanced the muzzle of the gun and took a stride forward at the same moment.

"Hello!" he growled. "Be you crazy, too? What in all git out be you traipsing through these woods for in the rain?"

# CHAPTER XI

## MR. PETERBY PAUL AND "WHOSIS"

Ruth Fielding was more than a little startled, for the appearance of this bearded and gruff-spoken man was much against him.

She had become familiar, however, during the past months with all sorts and conditions of men—many of them much more dangerous looking than this stranger.

Her experiences at the battlefront in France had taught her many things. Among them, that very often the roughest men are the most tender with and considerate of women. Ruth knew that the girls and women working in the Red Cross and the "Y" and the Salvation Army might venture among the roughest *poilus*, Tommies and our own Yanks without fearing insult or injury.

After that first startled "Oh!" Ruth Fielding gave no sign of fearing the bearded man with the gun under his arm. She stood her ground as he approached her.

"How many air there of ye, Sissy?" he wanted to know. "And air ye all loose from some bat factory? That other one's crazy as all git out."

Alice B. Emerson

"Oh, did you see her?"

"If ye mean that Whosis that's wanderin' around yellin' like a cat-o'-mountain—"

"Oh, dear! It was she that was screaming so!"

"I should say it was. I tried to cotch her—"

"And that scared her more, I suppose."

"Huh! Be I so scareful to look at?" the stranger demanded. "Or, mebbe *you* ain't loony, lady?"

"I should hope not," rejoined Ruth, beginning to laugh.

"Then how in tarnation," demanded the bearded man, "do you explain your wanderin' about these woods in this storm?"

"Why," said Ruth, "I was trying to catch that poor creature, too."

"That Whosis?" he exclaimed.

"Whatever and whoever she is. See! Here's one of her shoes."

"Do tell! She's lost it, ain't she? Don't you reckon she's loony?"

"It may be that she is out of her mind. But she couldn't hurt you—a big, strong man like you."

"That's as may be. I misdoubted me she was some kind of a Whosis," said the woodsman. "I seen her a couple of times and heard her holler ev'ry time the lightning was real sharp."

"The poor creature has been frightened half to death by the tempest," said Ruth.

"Mebbe. But where did she come from? And where did you come from, if I may ask? This yere ain't a neighborhood that many city folks finds their way into, let me tell ye."

Ruth told him her name and related the mishap that had happened to the two cars at the bottom of the hill.

"Wal, I want to know!" he responded. "Out o' gasoline, heh? Wal, that can be mended."

"Tom Cameron has gone on foot for some."

"Which way did he go, Ma'am?"

"East," she said, pointing.

"Towards Ridgeton? Wal, he'll have a fine walk."

"But we have not seen any gasoline sign for ever so far back on the road."

"That's right. Ain't no reg'lar place. But I guess I might be able to scare up enough gas to help you folks out. Ye see, we got a saw mill right up this gully and we got a gasoline engine to run her. I'm a-watchin' the place till the gang come in to work next month. That there Whosis got me out in the rain—"

"Oh! Where do you suppose the poor thing has gone?" interrupted Ruth. "We should do something for her."

"Wal, if she don't belong to you folks—"

Alice B. Emerson

"She doesn't. But she should not be allowed to wander about in this awful way. Is she a woman grown, or a child?"

"I couldn't tell ye. I ain't been close enough to her. By the way, my name is Peterby Paul, and I'm well and fav'rably knowed about this mounting. I did have my thoughts about you, same as that Whosis, I must say. But you 'pear to be all right. Wait, and I'll bring ye down a couple of cans of gasoline, and you can go on and pick up the feller that's started to walk to Ridgeton."

"But that poor creature I followed up here, Mr. Paul? We *must* find her."

"You say she ain't nothin' to you folks?"

"But she is alone, and frightened."

"Wal, I expect so. She did give me a start for fair. I don't know where she could have come from 'nless she belongs over toward Ridgeton at old Miz Abby Drake's. She's got some city folks stopping with her—"

"There she is!" cried Ruth, under her breath.

A hobbling figure appeared for a moment on the side of the ravine. The rain had ceased now, but it still dripped plentifully from the trees.

"I'm going after her!" exclaimed Ruth.

"All right, Ma'am," said Mr. Peterby Paul. "I guess she ain't no Whosis, after all."

Ruth could run much faster than the strange person who had so startled both the woodsman and herself. And running lightly, the girl of the Red Mill was almost at her quarry's elbow before her presence was suspected by the latter.

The woman turned her face toward Ruth and screeched in evident alarm. She looked wild enough to be called a "Whosis," whatever kind of supernatural apparition that might be. Her silk dress was in rags; her hair floated down her back in a tangled mane; altogether she was a sorry sight, indeed.

She was a woman of middle age, dark, slight of build, and of a most pitiful appearance.

"Don't be frightened! Don't be afraid of me," begged Ruth. "Where are your friends? I will take you to them."

"It is the voice of God," said the woman solemnly. "I am wicked. He will punish me. Do you know how wicked I am?" she added in a tense whisper.

"I have no idea," Ruth replied calmly. "But I think that when we are nervous and distraught as you are, we magnify our sins as well as our troubles."

Really, Ruth Fielding felt that she might take this philosophy to herself. She had been of late magnifying her troubles, without doubt.

"I have been a great sinner," said the woman. "Do you know, I used to steal my little sister's bread and jam. And now she is dead. I can never make it up to her."

Plainly this was a serious matter to the excited mind of the poor woman.

"Come on down the hill with me. I have got an automobile

Alice B. Emerson

there and we can ride to Mrs. Drake's in it. Isn't that where you are stopping?"

"Yes, yes. Abby Drake," said the lost woman weakly. "We— we all started out for huckleberries. And I never thought before how wicked I was to my little sister. But the storm burst—such a terrible storm!" and the poor creature cowered close to Ruth as the thunder muttered again in the distance.

"It is the voice of God—"

"Come along!" urged Ruth. "Lots of people have made the same mistake. So Aunt Alvirah says. They mistake some other noise for the voice of God!"

The woman was now so weak that the strong girl could easily lead her. Mr. Peterby Paul looked at the forlorn figure askance, however.

"You can't blame me for thinkin' she was a Whosis," he said to Ruth. "Poor critter! It's lucky you came after her. She give me such a start I might o' run sort o' wild myself."

"Perhaps if you had tried to catch her it would only have made her worse," Ruth replied, gently patting the excited woman's hand.

"The voice of God!" muttered the victim of her own nervousness.

"And she traipsing through these woods in a silk dress!" exclaimed Mr. Paul. "I tell 'em all, city folks ain't got right good sense."

"Maybe you are right, Mr. Paul," sighed Ruth. "We are all a little queer, I guess. I will take her down to the car."

"And I'll be right along with a couple of cans of gasoline, Ma'am," rejoined Peterby Paul. "Ain't no use you and your friends bein' stranded no longer."

"If you will be so kind," Ruth said.

He turned back up the ravine and Ruth urged the lost woman down the hill. The poor creature was scarcely able to walk, even after she had put on her lost shoe. Her fears which had driven her into this quite irresponsible state, were the result of ungoverned nervousness. Ruth thought seriously of this fact as she aided her charge down the hillside.

She must steady her own nerves, or the result might be quite as serious. She had allowed the loss of her scenario to shake her usual calm. She knew she had not been acting like herself during this automobile journey and that she had given her friends cause for alarm.

Then and there Ruth determined to talk no more about her loss or her fears regarding the missing scenario. If it was gone, it was gone. That was all there was to it. She would no longer worry her friends and disturb her own mental poise by ruminating upon her misfortune.

When she and the lost woman got out of the ravine, Ruth could hear the girls calling her. And there was Colonel Marchand's horizon-blue uniform in sight as he toiled up the ascent, looking for her.

"Don't be frightened, dear," Ruth said to the startled woman. "These are my friends."

Then she called to Helen that she was coming. Colonel Marchand hurried forward with an amazed question.

"Never mind! Don't bother her," Ruth said. "The poor creature has been through enough—out in all this storm, alone. We must get her to where she is stopping as soon as possible. See the condition her clothes are in!"

"But, Mademoiselle Ruth!" gasped the Frenchman. "We are stalled until Captain Tom comes back with the gasoline—is it not?"

"We are going to have gas in a very few minutes," returned Ruth gaily. "I did more than find this poor woman up on the hill. Wait!"

Helen and Jennie sprang at Ruth like a pair of terriers after a cat, demanding information and explanation all in a breath. But when they realized the state of mind of the strange woman, they calmed down.

They wrapped her in a dry raincoat and put her in the back of the big car. She remained quietly there with Jennie's Aunt Kate while Ruth related her adventure with Mr. Peterby Paul and the "Whosis."

"Goodness!" gasped Helen, "I guess he named her rightly. There must be something altogether wrong with the poor creature to make her wander about these wet woods, screeching like a loon."

"I'd screech, too," said Jennie Stone, "if I'd torn a perfectly good silk dress to tatters as she has."

"Think of going huckleberrying in a frock like that," murmured Ruth. "I guess you are both right. And Mr. Peterby Paul did have good reason for calling her a 'Whosis'."

# CHAPTER XII

## ALONGSHORE

Mr. Peterby Paul appeared after a short time striding down the wooded hillside balancing a five-gallon gasoline can in either hand.

"I reckon you can get to Ridgeton on this here," he said jovially. "Guess I'd better set up a sign down here so's other of you autermobile folks kin take heart if ye git stuck."

"You are just as welcome as the flowers in spring, tra-la!" cried Helen, fairly dancing with delight.

"You are an angel visitor, Mr. Paul," said the plump girl.

"I been called a lot o' things besides an angel," the bearded woodsman said, his eyes twinkling. "My wife, 'fore she died, had an almighty tart tongue."

"And *now*?" queried Helen wickedly.

"Wal, wherever the poor critter's gone, I reckon she's l'arned to bridle her tongue," said Mr. Peterby Paul cheerfully. "Howsomever, as the feller said, that's another day's job. Mr. Frenchy, let's pour this gasoline into them tanks."

Alice B. Emerson

Ruth insisted upon paying for the gasoline, and paying well. Then Peterby Paul gave them careful directions as to the situation of Abby Drake's house, at which it seemed the lost woman must belong.

"Abby always has her house full of city folks in the summer," the woodsman said. "She is pretty near a Whosis herself, Abby Drake is."

With which rather unfavorable intimation regarding the despised "city folks," Mr. Peterby Paul saw them start on over the now badly rutted road.

Helen drove the smaller car with Ruth sitting beside her. Henri Marchand took the wheel of the touring car, and the run to Boston was resumed.

"But we must not over-run Tom," said Ruth to her chum. "No knowing what by-path he might have tried in search of the elusive gasoline."

"I'll keep the horn blowing," Helen said, suiting action to her speech and sounding a musical blast through the wooded country that lay all about. "He ought to know his own auto-horn."

The tone of the horn was peculiar. Ruth could always distinguish it from any other as Tom speeded along the Cheslow road toward the Red Mill. But then, she was perhaps subconsciously listening for its mellow note.

She tacitly agreed with Helen, however, that it might be a good thing to toot the horn frequently. And the signal brought to the roadside an anxious group of women at a sprawling farmhouse not a mile beyond the spot where the two cars had been stalled.

"That is the Drake place. It must be!" Ruth exclaimed, putting out a hand to warn Colonel Marchand that they were about to halt.

A fleshy woman with a very ruddy face under her sunbonnet came eagerly out into the road, leading the group of evidently much worried women.

"Have you folks seen anything of—"

"*Abby!*" shrieked the woman Ruth had found, and she struggled to get out of the car.

"Well, I declare, Mary Marsden!" gasped the sunbonneted woman, who was plainly Abby Drake. "If you ain't a sight!"

"I—I'm so scared!" quavered the unforunate victim of her own nerves, as Ruth ran back to help her out of the touring car. "God is going to punish me, Abby."

"I certainly hope He will," declared her friend, in rather a hard-hearted way. "I told you, you ought to be punished for wearing that dress up there into the berry pasture, and—Land's sakes alive! Look at her dress!"

Afterward, when Ruth had been thanked by Mrs. Drake and the other women, and the cars were rolling along the highway again, the girl of the Red Mill said to Helen Cameron:

"I guess Tom is more than half right. Altogether, the most serious topic of conversation for all kinds and conditions of female humans is the matter of dress—in one way or another."

"How dare you slur your own sex so?" demanded Helen.

"Well, look at this case," her chum observed. "This Mary Marsden had been lost in the storm and killed for all they knew, yet Abby Drake's first thought was for the woman's dress."

"Well, it was a pity about the dress," Helen remarked, proving that she agreed with Abby Drake and the bulk of womankind—as her twin brother oft and again acclaimed.

Ruth laughed. "And now if we could see poor dear Tommy—"

The car rounded a sharp turn in the highway. The Drake house was perhaps a mile behind. Ahead was a long stretch of rain-drenched road, and Helen instantly cried:

"There he is!"

The figure of Tom Cameron with the empty gasoline can in his hand could scarcely be mistaken, although he was at least a mile in advance. Helen began to punch the horn madly.

"He'll know that," Ruth cried. "Yes, he looks back! Won't he be astonished?"

Tom certainly was amazed. He proceeded to sit down on the can and wait for the cars to overtake him.

"What are you traveling on?" he shouted, when Helen stopped with the engine running just in front of him. "Fairy gasoline?"

"Why, Tommy, you're not so smart!" laughed his sister. "It takes Ruth to find gas stations. We were stalled right in front of one, and you did not know it. Hop in here and take my place and I'll run back to the other car. Ruth will tell you all about it."

"Perhaps we had better let Colonel Marchand and Jennie have this honeymoon car," Ruth said doubtfully.

"Humph!" her chum observed, "I begin to believe it will be just as much a honeymoon car with you and Tom in it as with that other couple. 'Bless you, my children!'"

She ran back to the big car with this saucy statement. Tom grinned, slipped behind the wheel, and started the roadster slowly.

"It must be," he observed in his inimitable drawl, "that Sis has noticed that I'm fond of you, Ruthie."

"Quite remarkable," she rejoined cheerfully. "But the war isn't over yet, Tommy-boy. And if our lives are spared we've got to finish our educations and all that. Why, Tommy, you are scarcely out of short pants, and I've only begun to put my hair up."

"Jimminy!" he grumbled, "you do take all the starch out of a fellow. Now tell me how you got gas. What happened?"

Everybody has been to Boston, or expects to go there some time, so it is quite immaterial what happened to the party while at the Hub. They only remained two days, anyway, then they started off alongshore through the pleasant old towns that dot the coast as far as Cape Ann.

They saw the ancient fishing ports of Marblehead, Salem, Gloucester and Rockport, and then came back into the interior and did not see salt water again until they reached Newburyport at the mouth of the Merrimac.

The weather remained delightfully cool and sunshiny after that heavy tempest they had suffered in the hills, and they reached Portsmouth and remained at a hotel for three days when it rained again. The young folks chafed at this delay, but Aunt Kate declared that a hotel room was restful after jouncing over all sorts of roads for so long.

"They never will build a car easy enough for auntie," Jennie Stone declared. "I tell pa he must buy some sort of airship for us—"

"Never!" cried Aunt Kate in quick denial. "Whenever I go up in the air it will be because wings have sprouted on my shoulder blades. And I should not call an aeroplane easy riding, in any case."

"At least," grumbled Tom, "you can spin along without any trouble with country constables, and *that's* a blessing."

For on several occasions they had had arguments with members of the police force, in one case helping to support a justice and a constable by paying a fine.

They did not travel on Sunday, however, when the constables reap most of their harvest, so they really had little to complain of in that direction. Nor did they travel fast in any case.

After the rainy days at Portsmouth, the automobile party ran on with only minor incidents and no adventures until they reached Portland. There Ruth telegraphed to Mr. Hammond that they were coming, as in her letter, written before they left Cheslow, she had promised him she would.

Herringport, the nearest town to the moving picture camp at Beach Plum Point, was at the head of a beautiful harbor, dotted with islands, and with water as blue as that of the Bay of Naples. When the two cars rolled into this old seaport the party was welcomed in person by Mr. Hammond, the president and producing manager of the Alectrion Film Corporation.

"I have engaged rooms for you at the hotel here, if you want them," he told Ruth, after being introduced to Aunt Kate and Colonel Marchand, the only members of the party whom he had not previously met.

"But I can give you all comfortable bunks with some degree of luxury at the camp. At least, we think it luxurious after our gold mining experience in the West. You will get better cooking at the Point, too."

"But a camp!" sighed Aunt Kate. "We have roughed it so much coming down here, Mr. Hammond."

"There won't be any black ants at this camp," said her niece cheerfully.

"Only sand fleas," suggested the wicked Tom.

"You can't scare me with fleas," said Jennie. "They only hop; they don't wriggle and creep."

"My star in the 'Seaside Idyl,' Miss Loder, demanded hotel accommodations at first. But she soon changed her mind," Mr. Hammond said. "She is now glad to be on the lot with the rest of the company."

"It sounds like a circus," Aunt Kate murmured doubtfully.

"It is more than that, my dear Madam," replied the manager, laughing. "But these young people—"

"If Aunt Kate won't mind," said Ruth, "let us try it, while she remains at the Herringport Inn."

"I'll run her back and forth every day for the 'eats'," Tom promptly proposed.

"My duty as a chaperon—" began the good woman, when her niece broke in with:

"In numbers there is perfect safety, Auntie. There are a whole lot of girls down there at the Point."

"And we have chaperons of our own, I assure you," interposed Mr. Hammond, treating Aunt Kate's objection seriously. "Miss Loder has a cousin who always travels with her. Our own Mother Paisley, who plays character parts, has daughters of her own and is a lovely lady. You need not fear, Madam, that the conventions will be broken."

"We won't even crack 'em, Aunt Kate," declared Helen rouguishly. "I will watch Jen like a cat would a mouse."

"Humph!" observed the plump girl, scornfully. "*This* mouse, in that case, is likely to swallow the cat!"

# CHAPTER XIII

## THE HERMIT

"Now, tell me, Miss Ruth," said Mr. Hammond, having taken the girl of the Red Mill into his own car for the short run to Beach Plum Point, "what is this trouble about your new scenario? You have excited my curiosity during all these months about the wonderful script, and now you say it is not ready for me."

"Oh, Mr. Hammond!" exclaimed Ruth, "I fear it will never be ready for you."

"Nonsense! Don't lose heart. You have merely come to one of those thank-you-ma'ams in story writing that all authors suffer. Wait. It will come to you."

"No, no!" sighed Ruth. "It is nothing like that. I had finished the scenario. I had it all just about as I wanted it, and then—"

"Then what?" he asked in wonder at her emotion.

"It—it was stolen!"

"Stolen?"

"Yes. And all my notes—everything! I—I can't talk about it. And I never could write it again," sobbed Ruth. "It is the best thing I ever did, Mr. Hammond."

"If it is better than 'The Heart of a Schoolgirl', or 'The Forty-Niners', or 'The Boys of the Draft', then it must be some scenario, Miss Ruth. The last two are still going strong, you know. And I have hopes of the 'Seaside Idyl' catching the public fancy just when we are all getting rather weary of war dramas.

"If you can only rewrite this new story—"

"But Mr. Hammond! I am sure it has been stolen by somebody who will make use of it. Some other producer may put it on the screen, and then my version would fall flat—if no worse."

"Humph! And you have been so secret about it!"

"I took your advice, Mr. Hammond. I have told nobody about it—not a thing!"

"And somebody unknown stole it?"

"We think it was a vagrant actor. A tramp. Just the sort of person, though, who would know how to make use of the script."

"Humph! All actors were considered 'vagrants' under the old English law—in Shakespeare's younger days, for instance," remarked Mr. Hammond.

"You see how unwise it would be for me to try to rewrite the story—even if I could—and try to screen it."

"I presume you are right. Yes. But I hoped you would bring a story with you that we could be working on at odd times. I have a good all-around company here on the lot."

"I had most of your principals in mind when I wrote my scenario," sighed Ruth. "But I could not put my mind to that same subject now. I am discouraged, Mr. Hammond."

"I would not feel that way if I were you, Miss Ruth," he advised, trying, as everybody else did, to cheer her. "You will get another good idea, and like all other born writers, you will just *have* to give expression to it. Meantime, of course, if I get hold of a promising scenario, I shall try to produce it."

"I hope you will find a good one, Mr. Hammond."

He smiled rather ruefully. "Of course, there is scarcely anybody on the lot who hasn't a picture play in his or her pocket. I was possibly unwise last week to offer five hundred dollars spot cash for a play I could make use of, for now I suppose there will be fifty to read. Everybody, from Jacks, the property man, to the old hermit, believes he can write a scenario."

"Who is the hermit?" asked Ruth, with some curiosity.

"I don't know. Nobody seems to know who he is about Herringport. He was living in an old fish-house down on the Point when we came here last week with the full strength of the company. And I have made use of the old fellow in your 'Seaside Idyl'.

"He seems to be a queer duck. But he has some idea of the art of acting, it seems. Director Jim Hooley is delighted with him. But they tell me the old fellow is scribbling all night in his hut. The scenario bug has certainly bit that old codger. He's out for my five hundred dollars," and the producing manager laughed again.

"I hope you get a good script," said Ruth earnestly. "But don't ask me to read any of them, Mr. Hammond. It does seem as though I never wanted to look at a scenario again!"

"Then you are going to miss some amusement in this case," he chuckled.

"Why so?"

"I tell you frankly I do not expect much from even those professional actors. It was my experience even before I went into the motion picture business that plays submitted by actors were always full of all the old stuff—all the old theatrical tricks and the like. Actors are the most insular people in existence, I believe. They know how plays should be written to fulfill the tenets of the profession; but invention is 'something else again'."

The young people who had motored so far were welcomed by many of Mr. Hammond's company who had acted in "The Forty-Niners" and had met Ruth and her friends in the West, as related in "Ruth Fielding in the Saddle."

The shacks that had been built especially for the company's use were comfortable, even if they did smell of new pine boards. The men of the company lived in khaki tents. There were several old fish-houses that were likewise being utilized by the members of the company.

Beach Plum Point was the easterly barrier of sand and rock that defended the beautiful harbor from the Atlantic breakers. It was a wind-blown place, and the moan of the surf on the outer reef was continually in the ears of the campers on the Point.

The tang of salt in the air could always be tasted on the lips when one was out of doors. And the younger folks were out on the sands most of the time when they were not working, sleeping, or eating.

"We are going to have some fun here," promised Tom Cameron to Ruth, after their party had got established with its baggage. "See that hard strip of beach? That's no clamflat. I am going to race my car on that sand. Palm Beach has nothing on this. Jackman, the property man (you remember Jacks, don't you, Ruth?), says the blackfish and bass are biting off the Point. You girls can act in movies if you like, but *I* am going fishing."

"Don't talk movies to me," sighed the girl. "I almost wish we had not come, Tom."

"Nonsense! You shall go fishing with me. Put on your oldest duds and—well, maybe you will have to strip off your shoes and stockings. It is both wet and slippery on the rocks."

"Pooh! I'll put on my bathing suit and a sweater. I never was afraid of water yet," Ruth declared.

This was the morning after their arrival. Tom had been up to the port and brought down Aunt Kate for the day. Aunt Kate sat under an umbrella near where the company was working on location, and she scribbled all day in a notebook. Jennie whispered that she, too, was bitten by the scenario bug!

"I feel it coming over me," announced Helen. "I've got what I think is a dandy idea."

Alice B. Emerson

"Oh, there's too much to do," Jennie Stone said. "I couldn't find time to dabble in literature."

"My, oh, my!" gasped Helen, with scorn. "How busy we are! You and Henri spend all your time making eyes at each other."

"But just think, Nell!" cried the plump girl. "He's got to go back to France and fight—"

"And so has my Tom."

"But Tom is only your brother."

"And Henri is nothing at all to you," rejoined Helen cruelly. "A fiance is only an expectation. You may change your mind about Henri."

"Never!" cried Jennie, with horror.

"Well, he keeps you busy, I grant. And there go Tom and Ruth mooning off together with fish lines. Lots of fishing *they* will do! They are almost as bad as you and Henri. Why!" ejaculated Helen in some heat, "I am just driven to writing scenarios to keep from dying of loneliness."

"I notice that 'juvenile lead,' Mr. Simmons, is keeping you quite busy," remarked Jennie slyly, as she turned away.

It was a fact that Ruth and Tom enjoyed each others' company. But Helen need not have been even a wee bit jealous. To tell the truth, she did not like to "get all mussed up," as she expressed it, by going fishing. To Ruth the adventure was a glad relief from worriment. Much as she tried, she could not throw off all thought of her lost scenario.

She welcomed every incident that promised amusement and mental relaxation. Some of the troupe of actors—the men, mostly—were bathing off the Point.

"And see that man in the old skiff!" cried Ruth. "'The Lone Fisherman'."

The individual in question sat upon a common kitchen chair in the skiff with a big, patched umbrella to keep the sun off, and was fishing with a pole that he had evidently cut in the woods along the shore.

"That is that hermit fellow," said Tom. "He's a queer duck. And the boys bother him a good deal."

He was angrily driving some of the swimmers away from his fishing location at that moment. It was plain the members of the moving picture company used the hermit as a butt for their jokes.

While one fellow was taking up the hermit's attention in front, another bather rose silently behind him and reached into the bottom of the skiff. What this second fellow did Tom and Ruth could not see.

"The old chap can't swim a stroke," explained one of the laughing bathers to the visitors. "He's as afraid of water as a cat. Now you watch."

But Tom and Ruth saw nothing to watch. They went on to the tip of the Point and Tom prepared the fishing tackle and baited the hooks. Just as Ruth made her first cast there sounded a scream from the direction of the lone fisherman.

"What is it?" she gasped, dropping her pole.

The bathers had deserted the old man in the skiff, and were now at some distance. He was anchored in probably twenty feet of water.

To the amazement of Ruth and her companion, the skiff had sunk until its gunwales were scarcely visible. The hermit had wrenched away his umbrella and was now balanced upon the chair on his feet, in danger of sinking. His fear of this catastrophe was being expressed in unstinted terms.

# CHAPTER XIV

## A QUOTATION

"Do help him, Tom!" cried Ruth Fielding, and she started for the spot where the man and the skiff were sinking.

Tom cast aside his sweater, kicked his sneakers off, and plunged into the tide. Ruth was quite as lightly dressed as Tom; but she saw that he could do all that was necessary.

That was, to bring the frightened man ashore. This "hermit" as they called him, was certainly very much afraid of the water.

He splashed a good deal, and Tom had to speak sharply to keep him from getting a strangle-hold about his own neck.

"Jimminy! but that was a mean trick," panted Tom, when he got ashore with the fisherman. "Somebody pulled the plug out of the bottom of the skiff and first he knew, he was going down."

"It is a shame," agreed Ruth, looking at the victim of the joke curiously.

He was a thin-featured, austere looking man, scrupulously

Alice B. Emerson

shaven, but with rather long hair that had quite evidently been dyed. Now that it was plastered to his crown by the salt water (for he had been completely immersed more than once in his struggle with Tom Cameron) his hair was shown to be quite thin and of a greenish tinge at the roots.

The shock of being dipped in the sea so unexpectedly was plainly no small one for the hermit. He stood quite unsteadily on the strand, panting and sputtering.

"Young dogs! No respect for age and ability in this generation. I might have been drowned."

"Well, it's all over now," said Tom comfortingly. "Where do you live?"

"Over yonder, young man," replied the hermit, pointing to the ocean side of the point.

"We will take you home. You lie down for a while and you will feel better," Ruth said soothingly. "We will come back here afterward and get your skiff ashore."

"Thank you, Miss," said the man courteously.

"I'll make those fellows who played the trick on you get the boat ashore," promised Tom, running for his shoes and sweater.

The hermit proved to be a very uncommunicative person. Ruth tried to get him to talk about himself as they crossed the rocky spit, but all that he said of a personal nature was that his name was "John."

His shack was certainly a lonely looking hovel. It faced the tumbling Atlantic and it seemed rather an odd thing to Ruth that a man who was so afraid of the sea should have selected such a spot for his home.

The hermit did not invite them to enter his abode. He promised Ruth that he would make a hot drink for himself and remove his wet garments and lie down. But he only seemed moderately grateful for their assistance, and shut the door of the shack promptly in their faces when he got inside.

"Just as friendly as a sore-headed dog," remarked Tom, as they went back to the bay side of the Point.

"Perhaps the others have played so many tricks on him that he is suspicious of even our assistance," Ruth said.

Thus speaking, she stooped to pick up a bit of paper in the path. It had been half covered by the sand and might have lain there a long time, or only a day.

Just why this bit of brown wrapping paper had caught her attention, it would be hard to say. Ruth might have passed it a dozen times without noticing it.

But now she must needs turn the paper over and over in her hands as she watched Tom, with the help of the rather abashed practical jokers, haul the water-logged skiff ashore.

She had forgotten the fishing poles they had abandoned on the rocks, and sat down upon a boulder. Suddenly she discovered that there was writing on the bit of paper she had picked up. It was then that her attention really became fixed upon her find.

The characters had been written with an indelible pencil. The dampness had only blurred the writing instead of erasing it. Her attention thus engaged, she idly scrutinized more than the blurred lines. Her attitude as she sat there on the boulder slowly stiffened; her gaze focused upon the paper.

"Why! what is it?" she murmured at last.

The blurred lines became clearer to her vision. It was the wording of the phrase rather than the handwriting that enthralled her. This that follows was all that was written on the paper:

"Flash:—

"As in the beginning, is now, and ever shall be—"

To the ordinary observer, with no knowledge of what went before or followed this quotation, the phrase must seem idle. But the word "flash" is used by scenario writers and motion picture makers, indicating an explanatory phrase thrown on the screen.

And this quoted phrase struck poignantly to Ruth Fielding's mind. For it was one she had used in that last scenario—the one that had so strangely disappeared from the summer-house back at the Red Mill!

Amazed—almost stunned—by this discovery, she sat on the boulder scarcely seeing what Tom and the others were doing toward salvaging the old hermit's skiff and other property.

Thoughts regarding the quotation shuttled back and forth in the girl's mind in a most bewildering way. The practical side of her character pointed out that there really could be no significance in this discovery. It could not possibly have anything to do with her stolen script.

Yet the odd phrase, used in just this way, had been one of the few "flashes" indicated in her scenario. Was it likely that anybody else, writing a picture, would use just that phrase?

She balanced the improbability of this find meaning anything at all to her against the coincidence of another author using the quotation in writing a scenario. She did not know what to think. Which supposition was the more improbable?

The thought was preposterous that the paper should mean anything to her. Ruth was about to throw it away; and then, failing to convince herself that the quotation was but idly written, she tucked the piece of paper into the belt of her bathing suit.

When Tom was ready to go back to their fishing station, Ruth went with him and said nothing about the find she had made.

They had fair luck, all told, and the chef at the camp produced their catch in a dish of boiled tautog with egg sauce at dinner that evening. The company ate together at a long table, like a logging camp crew, only with many more of the refinements of life than the usual logging crew enjoys. It was, however, on a picnic plane of existence, and there was much hilarity.

These actor folk were very pleasant people. Even the star, Miss Loder, was quite unspoiled by her success.

"You know," she confessed to Ruth (everybody confided in Ruth), "I never would have been anything more than a stock actress in some jerkwater town, as we say in the West, if the movies hadn't become so popular. I have what they call the 'appealing face' and I can squeeze out real tears at the proper juncture. Those are two very necessary attributes for a girl who wishes to gain film success."

"But you can really act," Ruth said honestly. "I watched you to-day."

"I should be able to act. I come of a family who have been actors for generations. Acting is like breathing to me. But, of course, it is another art to 'register' emotion in the face, and very different from displaying one's feelings by action and audible expression. You know, one of our most popular present-day stage actresses got her start by an ability to scream off-stage. Nothing like that in the movies."

"You should hear Jennie Stone with a black ant down her back," put in Helen, with serious face. "I am sure Heavy could go the actress you speak of one better, and become even more popular."

"I am not to be blamed if I squeal at crawly things," sniffed the plump girl, hearing this. "See how brave I am in most other respects."

But that night Jennie exhibited what Tom called her "scarefulness" in most unmistakable fashion, and never again could she claim to be brave. She gave her chums in addition such a fright that they were not soon over talking about it.

The three college girls had cots in a small shack that Mr. Hammond had given up to their use. It was one of the shacks nearest the shore of the harbor. Several boat-docks near by ran out into the deep water.

It was past midnight when Jennie was for some reason aroused. Usually she slept straight through the night, and had to be awakened by violent means in time for breakfast.

She was not startled, but awoke naturally, and found herself broad awake. She sat up in her cot, almost convinced that it must be daylight. But it was the moon shining through a haze of clouds that lighted the interior of the shack. The other two girls were breathing deeply. The noises she heard did not at first alarm Jennie.

There was the whisper of the tide as it rolled the tiny pebbles and shells up the strand and, receding, swept them down again. It chuckled, too, among the small piers of the near-by docks.

Then the listening girl heard footsteps—or what she took to be that sound. They approached the shack, then receded. She began to be curious, then felt a tremor of alarm. Who could be wandering about the camp at this grim hour of the night?

She was unwise enough to allow her imagination to wake up, too. She stole from her bed and peered out of the screened window that faced the water. Almost at once a moving object met her frightened gaze.

It was a figure all in white which seemed to float down the lane between the tents and out upon the nearest boat-dock.

Afterward Jennie declared she could have suffered one of these spirit-looking manifestations in silence. She crammed the strings of her frilled nightcap between her teeth as a stopper!

This spectral figure was going away from the shack, anyway. It appeared to be bearing something in its arms. But then came a second ghost, likewise burdened. Gasping, Jennie waited, clinging to the window-sill for support.

A third spectre appeared, rising like Banquo's spirit at Macbeth's feast. This was too much for the plump girl's self-control. She opened her mouth, and her half-strangled shriek, the partially masticated cap-strings all but choking her, aroused Ruth and Helen to palpitating fright.

"Oh! What is it?" demanded Helen, bounding out of bed.

"Ghosts! Oh! Waw!" gurgled Jennie, and sank back into her friend's arms.

Helen was literally as well as mentally overcome. Jennie's weight carried her to the straw matting with a bump that shook the shack and brought Ruth, too, out of bed.

# CHAPTER XV

## AN AMAZING SITUATION

"'Ghost'?" cried Ruth Fielding. "Let me see it! Remember the campus ghost back at old Briarwood, Helen? I haven't seen a ghost since that time."

"Ugh! Get this big elephant off of me!" grunted her chum, impolitely as well as angrily. "*She's* no ghost, I do assure you. She's of the earth, earthy, and no mistake! Ouch! Get off, Heavy!"

"Oh! Oh! Oh!" groaned the plump girl. "I—I saw them. Three of them!"

"Sounds like a three-ring circus," snapped Helen.

But Ruth was peering through the window. She saw nothing, and complained thereof:

"Jen has had a nightmare. I don't see a thing."

"Nightmare, your granny!" sputtered the plump girl, finally rolling off her half crushed friend. "I saw it—them—*those*!"

"Your grammar is so mixed I wouldn't believe you on oath,"

Alice B. Emerson

declared Helen, getting to her own bare feet and paddling back to her cot for slippers and a negligee.

"O-o-oh, it is chilly," agreed Ruth, grabbing a wrap, too.

"Do tell us about it, Jennie," she begged. "Did you see your ghost through the window here?"

"It isn't my ghost!" denied the plump girl. "I'm alive, ain't I?"

"But you're not conscious," grumbled Helen.

"I can see!" wailed Jennie. "I haven't lost my eyesight."

"Stop!" Ruth urged. "Let us get at the foundation of this trouble. You say you saw—"

"I saw what I saw!"

"Oh, see-saw!" cried Helen. "We're all loony, now."

Ruth was about to ask another question, but she was again looking through the window. She suddenly bit off a cry of her own. She had to confess that the sight she saw was startling.

"Is—is that the ghost, Jennie?" she breathed, seizing the plump girl by her arm and dragging her forward.

Jennie gave one frightened look through the window and immediately clapped her palms over her eyes.

"Ow!" she wailed in muffled tones. "They're coming back."

They were, indeed! Three white figures in Indian file came stalking up the long dock. They approached the camp in a spectral procession and had she been awakened to see them first of all, Ruth might have been startled herself.

Helen peered over her chum's shoulder and in teeth-chattering monotone breathed in Ruth's ear the query:

"What is it?"

"It—it's Heavy's ghost."

"Not mine! Not mine!" denied the plump girl.

"Oh!" gasped Helen, spying the stalking white figures.

It was the moonlight made them appear so ghostly. Ruth knew that, of course, at once. And then—

"Who ever saw ghosts carrying garbage cans before?" ejaculated the girl of the Red Mill. "Mercy me, Heavy! do stop your wailing. It is the chef and his two assistants who have got up to dump the garbage on the out-going tide. What a perfect scare-cat you are!"

"You don't mean it, Ruth?" whimpered the plump girl. "Is that *all* they were?"

Helen began to giggle. And it covered her own fright. Ruth was rather annoyed.

"If you had remained in bed and minded your own business," she said to Jennie, "you would not have seen ghosts, or got us up to see them. Now go back to sleep and behave yourself."

"Yes, ma'am," murmured the abashed Jennie Stone. "How silly of me! I was never afraid of a cook before—no, indeed."

Alice B. Emerson

Helen continued to giggle spasmodically; but she fell asleep soon. As for Jennie, she began to breathe heavily almost as soon as her head touched the pillow. But Ruth must needs lie awake for hours, and naturally the teeth of her mind began to knaw at the problem of that bit of paper she had found in the sand.

The more she thought of it the less easy it was to discard the idea that the writing on the paper was a quotation from her own scenario script. It seemed utterly improbable that two people should use that same expression as a "flash" in a scenario.

Yet, if this paper was a connecting link between her stolen manuscript and the thief, *who was the thief?*

It would seem, of course, if this supposition were granted, that some member of the company of film actors Mr. Hammond had there at Beach Plum Point had stolen the scenario. At least, the stolen scenario must be in the possession of some member of the company.

Who could it be? Naturally Ruth considered this unknown must be one of the company who wished Mr. Hammond to accept and produce a scenario.

Ruth finally fell into a troubled sleep with the determination in her mind to take more interest in the proposed scenario-writing contest than she had at first intended.

She could not imagine how anybody could take her work and change it so that she would not recognize it! The plot of the story was too well wrought and the working out of it too direct.

She did not think that she had it perfect. Only that she had perfected the idea as well as she was able. But changing it would not hide from her the recognition of her own brain-child.

So after breakfast she went to Mr. Hammond to make inquiry about the scenario contest.

"Ha, ha! So you are coming to yourself, Miss Ruth!" he chuckled. "I told you you would feel different. I only wish *you* would get a real smart idea for a picture."

"Nothing like that!" she told him, shaking her head. "I could not think of writing a new scenario. You don't know what it means to me—the loss of that picture I had struggled so long with and thought so much about. I—

"But let us not talk of it," she hastened to add. "I am curious regarding the stories that have been offered to you."

"You need not fear competition," he replied. "Just as I told you, all these perfectly good acting people base their scenarios on dramas they have played or seen played. They haven't got the idea of writing for the screen at all, although they work before the camera."

"And that is no wonder!" exclaimed Ruth. "The way the directors take scenes, the actors never get much of an idea of the continuity of the story they are making. But these stories?"

"So far, I haven't found a possible scenario. And I have looked at more than a score."

"You don't mean it!"

"I most certainly do," he assured her. "Want to look at them?"

Alice B. Emerson

"Why—yes," confessed Ruth. "I am curious, as I tell you."

"Go to it!" exclaimed Mr. Hammond, opening a drawer of his desk and pointing to the pile of manuscripts within. "Consider yourself at home here. I am going over to the port with Director Hooley and most of the members of the company. We have found just the location for the shooting of that scene in your 'Seaside Idyl' where the ladies' aid society holds its 'gossip session' in the grove—remember?"

"Oh, yes," Ruth replied, not much interested, as she took the first scenario out of the drawer.

"And Hooley's found some splendid types, too, around the village. They really have a sewing circle connected with the Herringport Union Church, and I have agreed to help the ladies pay for having the church edifice painted if they will let us film a session of the society with our principal character actors mixed in with the local group. The sun is good to-day."

He went away, and a little later Ruth heard the automobiles start for Herringport. She had the forenoon to herself, for the rest of her party had gone out in a motor boat fishing—a party from which she had excused herself.

Eagerly she began to examine the scenarios submitted to Mr. Hammond. The possibility that she might find one of them near enough like her own lost story to suggest that it had been plagiarized, made Ruth's heart beat faster.

She could not forget the quotation on the scrap of brown paper. Somebody on this Point—and it seemed that the "somebody" must be one of the moving picture company—had written that quotation from her scenario. She felt that this could not be denied.

# CHAPTER XVI

## RUTH SOLVES ONE PROBLEM

Had Ruth Fielding been confronted with the question: "Did she expect to find a clue to the identity of the person who had stolen her scenario before she left the Red Mill?" she could have made no confident answer. She did not know what she would find when she sat down at Mr. Hammond's desk for the purpose of looking over the submitted stories.

Doubt and suspicion, however, enthralled her mind. She was both curious and anxious.

Ruth had no particular desire to read the manuscripts. In any case she did not presume Mr. Hammond desired her advice about selecting a script for filming.

She skimmed through the first story. It had not a thing in it that would suggest in the faintest way any familiarity of the author with her own lost scenario.

For two hours she fastened her attention upon one after another of the scenarios, often by main will-power, because of the utter lack of interest in the stories the writers had tried to put over.

Alice B. Emerson

Without being at all egotistical, Ruth Fielding felt confident that had any one of these scenario writers come into possession of her lost script, and been dishonest enough to use it, he would have turned out a much better story.

But not a trace of her original idea and its development was to be found in these manuscripts. Her suspicion had been needlessly roused.

Ruth could not deny that the scrap of paper found in the sand was quite as mysterious as ever. The quotation on it seemed to be taken directly from her own scenario. But there was absolutely nothing in this pile of manuscripts to justify her suspicions.

She was just as dissatisfied after scanning all the submitted scenarios as Mr. Hammond seemed to be with the day's work when the company came back from Herringport in the late afternoon.

"I suppose it is a sanguine disposition that keeps me at this game, Miss Ruth," he sighed. "I always expect much more than I can possibly get out of a situation; and when I fail I go on hoping just the same."

"I am sure that is a commendable disposition to possess," she laughed. "What has gone so wrong?"

"It is the old story of leading the horse to water, and the inability of making him drink. This is a balky horse, and no mistake!"

"Do tell me what you mean, Mr. Hammond?"

"Why, I told you we had got what the ladies call 'perfectly lovely' types for that scene to-day. You ought to see them,

Miss Ruth! You would be charmed. Just what the dear public expects a back-country sewing circle should look like."

"Oh!"

"And they all promised to be on hand at the location—and they were. I have had my experiences with amateurs before. I had begged the ladies to dress just as they would were they going to an actual meeting of their sewing society—"

"And they all dressed up?" laughed Ruth, clasping her hands.

"Well, that I expected to contend with. And most of them even in their best bib and tucker were not out of the picture. Not at all! That was not the main difficulty and the one that has spoiled our day's work."

"Indeed?"

"I am afraid Jim Hooley will have to fake the whole scene after all," continued the manager. "Those women came all dressed up 'to have their pictures took,' it is true. But the worst of it is, they could not be natural. It was impossible. They showed in every move and every glance that they were sitting with a bunch of actors and were not at all sure that what they were doing was altogether the right thing.

"We worked over them as though it were a 'mob scene' and there were five hundred in it instead of twenty. But twenty wooden dummies would have filmed no more unnaturally. You know, in your story, they are supposed to be discussing the bit of gossip about your heroine's elopement with the schoolteacher. I could not work up a mite of enthusiasm in their minds about such a topic."

Ruth laughed. But she saw that the matter was really serious for Mr. Hammond and the director. She became sympathetic.

"I fancy that if they had had a real scandal to discuss," she observed, "their faces would have registered more poignant interest."

"'Poignant interest'!" scoffed the manager in disgust. "If these Herringport tabbies had the toothache they would register only polite anguish—in public. They are the most insular and self-contained and self-suppressed women I ever saw. These Down-Easters! They could walk over fiery ploughshares and only wanly smile—"

Ruth went off into a gale of laughter at this. Mr. Hammond was a Westerner by birth, and he found the Yankee character as hard to understand as did Henri Marchand.

"Have you quite given up hope, Mr. Hammond?" Ruth asked.

"Well, we'll try again to-morrow. Oh, they promised to come again! They are cutting out rompers, or flannel undervests, I suppose, for the South Sea Island children; or something like that. They are interested in that job, no doubt.

"I wanted them to 'let go all holts,' as these fishermen say, and be eager and excited. They are about as eager as they would be doing their washing, or cleaning house—if as much!" and Mr. Hammond's disappointment became too deep for further audible expression.

Ruth suddenly awoke to the fact that one of her best scenes in the "Seaside Idyl" was likely to be spoiled. She talked with Mr. Hooley about it, and when the day's run was developed and run off in one of the shacks which was used for a try-out room, Ruth saw that the manager had not put the matter too strongly. The sewing circle scene lacked all that snap and go needed to make it a realistic piece of action.

Of course, there were enough character actors in the company to use in the scene; but naturally an actor caricatures such parts as were called for in this scene. The professional would be likely to make the characters seem grotesque. That was not the aim of the story.

"I thought you were not going to take any interest in this 'Seaside Idyl,' at all," suggested Helen, when Ruth was talking about the failure of the scene after supper that night.

"I can't help it. My reputation as a scenario writer is at stake, just as much as is Mr. Hooley's reputation as director," Ruth said, smiling. "I really didn't mean to have a thing to do with the old picture. But I can see that somebody has got to put a breath of naturalness into those ladies' aid society women, or this part of the picture will be a fizzle."

"And our Ruth," drawled Jennie, "is going to prescribe one of her famous cure-alls, is she?"

"I believe I can make them look less like a lot of dummies while they are cutting out rompers for cannibal island pickaninnies," laughed Ruth. "Tom, I am going to the port with you the first thing in the morning."

"By all means," said Captain Cameron. "I am yours to command."

Her newly aroused interest in the scenario at present being filmed, was a good thing for Ruth Fielding. Having found nothing at all in the submitted stories that suggested her own lost story, the girl of the Red Mill tried to put aside again the thing that so troubled her mind. And this new interest helped.

Alice B. Emerson

In the morning before breakfast she and Tom ran over to the port in the maroon roadster. While they were having breakfast at the inn, Ruth asked the waitress, who was a native of this part of the country, about the Union Church and some of the more intimate life-details of the members of its congregation.

It is not hard to uncover neighborhood gossip of a kind not altogether unkindly in any similar community. The Union Church had a new minister, and he was young. He was now away on his vacation, and more than one local beauty and her match-making mamma would have palpitation of the heart before he returned for fear that the young clergyman would have his heart interests entangled by some designing "foreigner."

Tom had no idea as to what Ruth Fielding was getting at through this questioning of the beaming Hebe who waited on them at breakfast. And he was quite as much in the dark as to his friend's motive when Ruth announced their first visit to be to the office of the Herringport *Harpoon*, the local news sheet.

# CHAPTER XVII

## JOHN, THE HERMIT'S, CONTRIBUTION

A man with bushy hair, a pencil stuck over his ear, and wearing an ink-stained apron, met them in the office of the *Harpoon*. This was Ezra Payne, editor and publisher of the weekly news-sheet, and this was his busiest day. The *Harpoon*, Ruth had learned, usually went into the mails on this day.

"Tut, tut! I see. Is this a joke?" Mr. Payne pursed his lips and wrinkled his brow in uncertainty.

"A whole edition, Miss? Wall, I dunno. I do have hard work selling all the edition some weeks. But I have reg'lar subscribers—"

"This will not interfere with your usual edition of the *Harpoon*," she hastened to assure him.

"How's that, Miss?"

"I want to buy an edition of one copy."

"One copy!"

Alice B. Emerson

"Yes, sir. I want something special printed in one paper. Then you can take it out and print your regular edition."

"Tut, tut! I see. Is this a joke?" Mr. Payne asked, his eyes beginning to twinkle.

"It is the biggest joke you ever heard of," declared Ruth.

"And who's the joke on?"

"Wait and see what I write," Ruth said, sitting down at the battered old desk where he labored over his editorials and proofsheets.

Opening a copy of the last week's *Harpoon* that lay there, she was able to see the whole face of the paper.

"I've got the inside run off," said Mr. Payne, still doubtfully. "So you can't run anything on the second and third pages."

"Oh, I want the most prominent place for my item," laughed Ruth. "Front page, top column—Here it is!"

He bent over her. Tom stared in wonder, too, as Ruth pointed to an item under a certain heading at the top of the middle column of the front page of the sheet.

"That is just where I want my item to appear," she said briskly to the editor. "You run that—that department there every week?"

"Oh, yes, Miss. The people expect it. You know how folks are. They look for those items first of all in a country paper."

"Yes. It is so. One of the New York dailies is still printed with that human foible in mind. It caters to this very curiosity that your *Harpoon* caters to."

"Yes, Miss. You're right. Most folks have the same curiosity, city or country. Shakespeare spoke of the 'seven ages of man'; but there are only three of particular interest—to womankind, anyway; and they are all *here*."

"There you go! Slurring the women," she laughed. "Or do you speak compliments?"

"I guess the women have it right," chuckled Mr. Payne. "Now, what is it you want me to print in one paper for you?"

Ruth drew a scratch pad to her and scribbled rapidly for a couple of minutes. Then she passed the page to the newspaper proprietor.

Mr. Payne read it, stared at her, pursed his lips, and then read it again. Suddenly he burst into a cackle of laughter, slapping his thigh in high delight.

"By gravy!" he chortled, "that's a good one on the dominie. By gravy! wait till I tell—"

"Don't you tell anybody, Mr. Payne," interrupted Ruth, smiling, but firmly. "I am buying your secrecy as well as your edition of *one copy*."

"I get you! I get you!" declared the old fellow. "This is to be on the q.t.?"

"Positively."

"You sit right here. The front page is all made up on the stone, Marriages, Births, Death Notices, and all. I'll set the paragraph and slip it in at the top o' the column. My boy is out, but this young man can help me lift the page into the press. She's all warmed up, and I was going to start printing when Edgar comes back from breakfast."

He grabbed the piece of copy and went off into the printing room, chuckling. Half an hour later the first paper came from the press, and Ruth and Tom bent over it. The item the girl had written was plainly printed in the position she had chosen on the front page of the *Harpoon*.

"Now, you are to keep still about this," Ruth said, threatening Mr. Payne with a raised finger.

"I don't know a thing about it," he promised, pocketing the bill she took from her purse, and in high good humor over the joke.

Tom helped him take the front page from the press again. The printer unlocked the chase, and removed and distributed the three lines he had set up at Ruth's direction.

The crowd from Beach Plum Point came over in the cars about noontime. Aunt Kate had remained at the inn on this morning, and she and Ruth walked to the "location," which was a beautiful old shaded front yard at the far end of the village.

Helen and Jennie had come with the real actors, and were to appear in the picture. The story related incidents at a Sunday-school picnic, and most of the comedy had already been filmed on the lot.

The scene around the long sewing table under the trees, when the ladies' aid was at work with needle and tongue, should be the principal incident of this reel devoted to the picnic.

The heroine, to the amazement of the village gossips, has run away with the schoolmaster and married him in the next county. A certain character in the picture runs in with this bombshell of news and explodes it in the midst of the group about the sewing table.

The day before this point had failed to make much impresssion upon the amateur members of the company engaged in this typical scene. The Herringport ladies were not at all interested in such a thing happening to the town's schoolmaster, for to tell the truth the local schoolmaster was an old married man with a house full of children and nothing at all romantic about him.

Ruth took Mr. Hooley aside and showed him the copy of the *Harpoon* she had had printed, and whispered to him her idea of the change in the action of the scenario. He seized upon the scheme—and the paper—with gusto.

"You are a jewel, Miss Fielding!" he declared. "If this doesn't make those old tabbies come to life and act naturally, nothing ever will!"

Ruth left the matter in the director's hands and retired from the location. She had no intention herself of appearing in the picture. She found Mr. Hammond sitting in his automobile in a state of good-humor.

"You seem quite sure that the work will go better to-day, Mr. Hammond," Ruth observed, with curiosity as to the reason for his apparent enjoyment.

"Whether it does or not, Miss Ruth," he responded. "There is something that I fancy is going to be more than a little amusing."

Alice B. Emerson

He tapped a package wrapped in a soiled newspaper which lay on the seat beside him. "Thank goodness, I can still enjoy a joke."

"What is the joke? Let me enjoy it, too," she said.

"With the greatest of pleasure. I'll let you read it, if you like—as you did those other scenarios."

"What! Is it a movie story?" she asked.

"So I am assured. It is the contribution of John, the hermit. He brought it to me just before we started over here this morning. Poor old codger! Just look here, Miss Ruth."

Mr. Hammond turned back the loose covering of the package on the automobile seat. Ruth saw a packet of papers, seemingly of roughly trimmed sheets of wrapping paper and of several sizes. At the top of the upper sheet was the title of the hermit's scenario. It was called "Plain Mary." She glanced down the page, noting that it was written in a large, upright, hand and with an indelible pencil.

Ruth Fielding had not the least idea that she was to take any particular interest in this picture-story. She smiled more because Mr. Hammond seemed so amused than for any other reason. Secretly she thought that most of these moving picture people were rather unkind to the strange old man who lived alone on the seaward side of the Beach Plum Point.

"Want to read it over?" Mr. Hammond asked her. "I would consider it a favor, for I've got to go back and try to catch up with my correspondence. I expect this is worse than those you skimmed through yesterday."

Ruth did not hear him. Suddenly she had seen something that had not at first interested her. She read the first few lines of the opening, and saw nothing in them of importance. It was the writing itself that struck her.

"Why!" she suddenly gasped.

She was reminded of something that she had seen before. This writing—

"Let me go back to the camp with you, Mr. Hammond," she said, slipping into the seat and taking the packet of written sheets into her lap. "I—I will look through this scenario, if you like. There is something down there on the Point that I want."

"Sure. Be glad to have your company," he said, letting in his clutch after pushing the starter. "We're off."

Ruth did not speak again just then. With widening eyes she began to devour the first pages of the hermit's manuscript.

Alice B. Emerson

# CHAPTER XVIII

## UNCERTAINTIES

The automobile purred along the shell road, past the white-sided, green-blinded houses of the retired ship captains and the other well-to-do people of Herringport. The car ran so smoothly that Ruth might have read all the way.

But after the first page or two—those containing the opening scenes of "Plain Mary"—she dared not read farther.

Not yet. It was not that there was a familiar phrase in the upright chirography of the old hermit. The story merely suggested a familiar situation to Ruth's mind. Thus far it was only a suggestion.

There was something else she felt she must prove or disprove first of all. She sat beside Mr. Hammond quite speechless until they came to the camp on the harbor shore of Beach Plum Point.

He went off cheerfully to his letter writing, and Ruth entered the shack she occupied with Helen and Jennie. She opened her locked writing-case. Under the first flap she inserted her fingers and drew forth the wrinkled scrap of paper she had picked up on the sands.

A glance at the blurred writing assured her that it was the same as that of the hermit's scenario.

"Flash:

"As in the beginning, is now, and ever shall be—"

Shakingly Ruth sat down before the cheap little maple table. She spread open the newspaper wrapper and stared again at the title page of "Plain Mary."

That title was nothing at all like the one she had given her lost scenario. But a title, after all, meant very little.

The several scenes suggested in the beginning of the hermit's story did not conflict with the plot she had evolved, although they were not her own. She had read nothing so far that would make this story different from her own. The names of the characters were changed and the locations for the first scene were different from those in her script. Nevertheless the action and development of the story might prove to be exactly like hers.

She shrank from going deeper into the hermit's script. She feared to find her suspicions true; yet she *must* know.

Finally she began to read. Page after page of the large and sprawling writing she turned over, face down upon the table. Ruth grew so absorbed in the story that she did not note the passing of time. She was truly aware of but one thing. And that seized upon her mind to wring from it both bitterness and anger.

"Want to go back to the port, Miss Ruth?" asked Mr. Hammond. "I want to mail my letters."

Alice B. Emerson

His question startled her. She sprang up, a spot of crimson in either cheek. Had he looked at her, the manager would certainly have noted her strange look.

"I'll come in a minute," she called to him in a half-stifled voice.

She laved her eyes and cheeks in cool water, removing such marks of her emotion as she could. Then she bundled up the hermit's scenario and joined Mr. Hammond in the car.

"Did you look at this?" she asked the producer as he started the motor.

"Bless you, no! What is it? As crazy as the old codger himself?"

"Do you really think that man is crazy?" she asked sharply.

"Why, I don't really know. Just queer perhaps. It doesn't seem as though a sane man would live all stark alone over on that sea-beaten point."

"He is an actor," declared Ruth. "Your director says so."

"At least, he does not claim to be, and they usually do, you know," chuckled Mr. Hammond. "But about this thing—"

"You read it! Then I will tell you something," said the girl soberly, and she refused to explain further.

"You amaze me," said the puzzled manager. "If that old codger has succeeded in turning out anything worth while, I certainly shall believe that 'wonders never cease.'"

"He has got you all fooled. He *is* a good actor," declared

Ruth bitterly. Then, as Mr. Hammond turned a puzzled frown upon her, she added, "Tell me what you think of the script, Mr. Hammond, before you speak to—er—John, or whatever his name may be."

"I certainly am curious now," he declared.

They got back to the place where the director had arranged to "shoot" the sewing circle scene just as everything was all set for it. Mother Paisley dominated the half circle of women about the long table under the trees. Ruth marveled at the types Mr. Hooley had found in the village. And she marveled further that any group of human beings could appear so wooden.

"Oh, Ruth!" murmured Helen, who was not in this scene, but was an interested spectator, "they will surely spoil the picture again. Poor Mr. Hooley! He takes *such* pains."

It was like playing a child's game for most of the members of the Herringport Union congregation. They were selfconscious, and felt that they were in a silly situation. Those who were not too serious of demeanor were giggling like schoolgirls.

Yet everything was ready for the cameras. Mr. Hooley's keen eye ran over all the group. He waved a hand to the camera men.

"Ready camera—action—go!"

The women remained speechless. They merely looked at each other in a helpless way. It was evident they had forgotten all the instructions the director had given them.

But suddenly into the focus of the cameras ran a barefooted

urchin waving a newspaper. This was the Alectrion Company's smartest "kid" actor and a favorite wherever his tousled head, freckled face, and wide grin appeared on the screen. He plunged right at Mother Paisley and thrust the paper into her hand, while he pointed at a certain place on the front page.

"Read *that*, Ma Bassett!" cried the news vender.

Mrs. Paisley gave expression first to wonder, then utter amazement, as she read the item Ruth had had inserted in this particular "edition" of the *Harpoon*. She was a fine old actress and her facial registering of emotion was a marvel. Mr. Hooley had seldom to advise her.

Now his voice was heard above the clack of the cameras:

"Pass it to the lady at your left. That's it! Cling to the paper. Get your heads together—three of you now!"

The amateur players looked at each other and began to grin. The scene promised to be as big a "fizzle" as the one shot the previous day.

But the woman next to Mrs. Paisley, after looking carelessly at the paper, of a sudden came to life. She seized the *Harpoon* with both hands, fairly snatching it out of the actress' hands. She was too startled to be polite.

"What under the canopy is this here?" she sputtered.

She was a small, wiry, vigorous woman, and she had an expressive, if a vinegary, face. She rose from her seat and forgot all about her "play-acting."

"What d'you think it says here?" she demanded of her sister-members of the ladies' aid.

"Sh!"

"Ella Painter, you're a-bustin' up the show!" admonished a motherly old person at the end of the table.

But Mrs. Painter did not notice these hushed remarks. She read the item in the paper aloud—and so extravagantly did she mouth the astonishing words that Ruth feared they might be read on her lips when shown on the screen.

"Listen!" Mrs. Painter cried. "Right at the top of the marriage notices! 'Garside—Smythe. At Perleyvale, Maine, on August twenty-second, the Reverend Elton Garside, of Herringport, and Miss Amy Smythe, of Perleyvale.' What do you know about that?"

The gasp of amazement that went up from the women of the Herringport Union Church was almost a chorus of anguish. The paper was snatched from hand to hand. Nobody could accuse the amateurs now of being "wooden."

Not until Mrs. Paisley in the character of *Ma Bassett*, at the signal from Mr. Hooley, fell back in her chair, exclaim-ing: "My mercy me! Luella Sprague and the teacher! Who'd have thought it?" did the company in general suspect that something had been "put over on them."

"All right! All right!" shouted Jim Hooley in high delight, stopping his camera men. "That's fine! It's great! Miss Fielding, your scheme worked like a charm."

The members of the sewing circle began to ask questions.

"Do you mean to say this is in the play?" demanded Mrs.

Ella Painter, waving the newspaper and inclined to be indignant.

"Yes, Mrs. Painter. That marriage notice is just a joke," the director told her. "It certainly gave you ladies a start and— Well, wait till you see this scene on the screen!"

"But ain't it *so*?" cried another. "Why, Mr. Garside— Why! it's in the *Harpoon*."

"But you won't find it in another *Harpoon*," laughed the director, recovering possession of the newspaper. "It's only a joke. But I positively had to give you ladies a real shock or we'd never have got this scene right."

"Well, of all the impudence!" began Mrs. Painter.

However, she joined in the laughter a minute later. At best, the women had won from Mr. Hammond enough money to pay for the painting of their church edifice, and they were willing to sacrifice their dignity for that.

## CHAPTER XIX

## COUNTERCLAIMS

"I declare, Ruth! that was a ridiculous thing to do," exclaimed Helen, when they were on their way back to the Point. "But it certainly brought the sewing circle women all up standing."

"I've been wondering all day what Ruth was up to," said Tom, who was steering the big car. "I was in on it without understanding her game."

"Well, it was just what the directer needed," chuckled Jennie. "Oh, it takes our Ruth to do things."

"I wonder?" sighed the girl of the Red Mill, in no responsive mood.

She had something very unpleasant before her that she felt she must do, and nothing could raise her spirits. She did not speak to anybody about the hermit's scenario. She waited for Mr. Hammond to express his opinion of it.

At the camp she found a letter for her from the doctor's wife who had promised to keep her informed regarding Arabella Montague Fitzmaurice Pike. That young person was doing well and getting fat at the Perkins' farm. But Mrs. Holmes was quite sure that she had not heard from her father.

"You've got another half-orphan on your hands, Ruth," said Helen. She made it a point always to object to Ruth's charities. "I don't believe that man will ever show up again. If he went away with a medicine show—"

"No, no," said Ruth firmly. "No child would ever respect and love her father as Bella does if he was not good to her. He will turn up."

Just then Tom called from outside the door of the girls' shack.

"What say to a moonlight dip off the Point?" he asked. "The tide is not very low. And I missed my splash this morning."

"We're with you, Tommy," responded his sister. "Wait till we get into bathing suits."

Even Ruth was enthusiastic—to a degree—over this. In twenty minutes they were running up the beach with Tom and Henri toward the end of the Point.

"Let's go over and get the surf," suggested Jennie. "I do love surf bathing. All you have to do is to bob up and down in one place."

"Heavy is lazy even in her sport," scoffed Helen. "But I'm game for the rough stuff."

They crossed the neck of land near the hermit's hut. There was a hard beach almost in front of the hut, and up this the breakers rolled and foamed delightfully. The so-called hermit, hearing their voices, came out and sat on a rock to watch them. But he did not offer to speak until Ruth went over to him.

"Mr. Hammond let me read your script, John," she said coldly.

"Indeed?" he rejoined without emotion.

"Where did you get the idea for that scenario?"

He tapped his head with a long forefinger. "Right inside of that skull. I do my own thinking," he said.

"You did not have any help about it? You originated the idea of 'Plain Mary?'"

He nodded. "You ain't the only person who can write a picture," he observed. "And I think that this one they are filming for you is silly."

Ruth stared down at him, but said nothing more. She was ready to go back to camp as soon as the others would, and she remained very silent. Mr. Hammond had been asking for her, Miss Loder said. When Ruth had got into something more presentable than a wet bathing suit, she went to his office.

"What do you know about this?" he demanded in plain amazement. "This story the old man gave me to read is a wonder! It is one of the best ideas I ever saw for the screen. Of course, it needs fixing up a bit, but it's great! What did you think of it, Miss Ruth?"

"I am glad you like it, Mr. Hammond," she said, steadying her voice with difficulty.

Alice B. Emerson

"I do like it, I assure you."

"It is *my* story, Mr. Hammond!" she exclaimed. "It is the very scenario that was stolen from me at home. He's just changed the names of the characters and given it a different title, and spoiled some of the scenes. But a large part of it is copied word for word from my manuscript!"

"Miss Fielding!" gasped the president of the Alectrion Film Corporation.

"I am telling you the truth," Ruth cried, rather wildly, it must be confessed, and then she broke down and wept.

"My goodness! It can't be possible! You—you've let your mind dwell upon your loss so much—"

"Do you think I am crazy?" she demanded, flaring up at him, her anger drying her tears.

"Certainly not," he returned gently; yet he looked at her oddly. "But mistakes have been made—"

"Mistakes, indeed! It is no mistake when I recognize my own work."

"But—but how could this old man have stolen your work—and away back there at the Red Mill? I believe he has lived here on the Point for years. At least, every summer."

"Then somebody else stole it and he got the script from them. I tell you it is mine!" cried Ruth.

"Miss Fielding! Let us be calm—"

"You would not be calm if you discovered somebody trying

to make use of something you had originated, and calling it theirs—no you wouldn't, Mr. Hammond!"

"But it seems impossible," he said weakly.

"That old man is an actor—an old-school actor. You can see that easily enough," she declared. "There was such a person about the Red Mill the day my script was lost. Oh, it's plain enough."

"Not so plain, Miss Ruth," said Mr. Hammond firmly. "And you must not make wild accusations. That will do no good—and may do harm in the end. It does not seem probable to me that this old hermit could have actually stolen your story. A longshore character like him—"

"He's not!" cried Ruth. "Don't you see that he is playing a part? He is no fisherman. No longshore character, as you call him, would be as afraid of the sea as he is. He is playing a part—and he plays it just as well as the parts Mr. Hooley gives him to play."

"Jove! There may be something in that," murmured the manager.

"He got my script some way, I tell you!" declared Ruth. "I am not going to let anybody maul my story and put it over as his own. No, sir!"

"But—but, Miss Ruth!" exclaimed Mr. Hammond. "How are you going to prove what you say is true?"

"Prove it?"

"Yes. You see, the burden of proof must be on you."

"But—but don't you believe me?" she murmured.

"Does it matter what I believe?" he asked her gently. "Remember, this man has entrusted me with a manuscript that he says is original. At least it is written in his own hand. I cannot go back of that unless you have some means of proof that his story is your story. Who did you tell about your plot, and how you worked it out? Did you read the finished manuscript—or any part of it—to any person who can corroborate your statements?"

"Oh, Mr. Hammond!" she cried, with sudden anguish in her voice. "Not a soul! Never to a single, solitary person. The girls, nor Aunt Alvirah, nor Tom—"

She broke down again and he could not soothe her. She wept with abandon, and Mr. Hammond was really anxious for her. He went to the door, whistled for one of the boys, and sent for Mrs. Paisley.

But Ruth recovered her composure—to a degree, at least—before the motherly old actress came.

"Don't tell anybody! Don't tell anybody!" she sobbed to Mr. Hammond. "They will think I am crazy! I haven't a word of proof. Only my word—"

"Against his," said the manager gravely. "I would accept your word, Miss Ruth, against the world! But we must have some proof before we deliberately accuse this old man of robbing you."

"Yes, yes. I see. I will be patient—if I can."

"The thing to do is to find out who this hermit really is," said Mr. Hammond. "Through discovering his private history we may put our finger on the thing that will aid you with proof. Good-night, my dear. Try to get calm again."

Alice B. Emerson

# CHAPTER XX

## THE GRILL

Ruth did not go back to her chums until, under Mother Paisley's comforting influence, she had recovered a measure of her self-possession. The old actress asked no questions as to the cause of Ruth's state of mind. She had seen too many hysterical girls to feel that the cause of her patient's breakdown was at all important.

"You just cry all you want to, deary. Right here on Mother Paisley's shoulder. Crying will do you good. It is the Good Lord's way of giving us women an outlet for all our troubles. When the last tear is squeezed out much of the pain goes with it."

Ruth was not ordinarily a crying girl. She had wept more of late, beginning with that day at the Red Mill when her scenario manuscript had been stolen, than in all her life before.

Her tears were now in part an expression of anger and indignation. She was as mad as she could be at this man who called himself "John, the hermit." For, whether he was the person who had actually stolen her manuscript, he very well knew that his scenario offered to Mr. Hammond was not original with him.

The worst of it was, he had mangled her scenario. Ruth could look upon it in no other way. His changes had merely muddied the plot and cheapened her main idea. She could not forgive that!

The other girls were drowsy when Ruth kissed Mother Paisley good-night and entered the small shack. She was glad to escape any interrogation. By morning she had gained control of herself, but her eyes betrayed the fact that she had not slept.

"You certainly do not look as though you were enjoying yourself down here," Tom Cameron said to her at breakfast time, and with suspicion. "Maybe we did come to the wrong place for our vacation after all. How about it, Ruth? Shall we start off in the cars again and seek pastures new?"

"Not now, Tom," she told him, hastily. "I must stay right here."

"Why?"

"Because—"

"That is no sensible reason."

"Let me finish," she said rather crossly. "Because I must see what sort of scenario Mr. Hammond finds—if he finds any— in this contest."

"Humph! And you said you and scenarios were done forever! I fancy Mr. Hammond is taking advantage of your good nature."

"He is not."

"You are positively snappish, Ruth," complained Tom. "You've changed your mind—"

"Isn't that a girl's privilege?"

"Very well, Miladi!" he said, with a deep bow as they rose from the table. "However, you need not give all your attention to these prize stories, need you? Let's do something besides follow these sun-worshippers around to-day."

"All right, Tommy-boy," acclaimed his sister. "What do you suggest?"

"A run along the coast to Reef Harbor where there are a lot of folks we know," Tom promptly replied.

"Not in that old *Tocsin*," cried Jennie. "She's so small I can't take off my sweater without tipping her over."

"Oh, what a whopper!" gasped Helen.

"Never mind," grinned her twin. "Let Jennie run to the superlatives if she likes. Anyway, I would not dream of going so far as the Harbor in that dinky little *Tocsin*. I've got my eye on just the craft, and I can get her over here in an hour by telephoning to the port. It's the *Stazy*."

"Goody!" exclaimed Jennie Stone. "That big blue yacht! And she's got a regular crew—and everything. Aunty won't be afraid to go with us in her."

"That's fine, Tom," said his sister with appreciation.

Even Ruth seemed to take some interest. But she suggested:

"Be sure there is gasoline enough, Tom. That *Stazy* doesn't spread a foot of canvas, and we are not likely to find a gas station out there in the ocean, the way we did in the hills of Massachusetts."

"Don't fear, Miss Fidget," he rejoined. "Are you all game?"

They were. The girls went to "doll up," to quote the slangy Tom, for Reef Harbor was one of the most fashionable of Maine coast resorts and the knockabout clothing they had been wearing at Beach Plum Point would never do at the Harbor hotels.

The *Stazy* was a comfortable and fast motor-yacht. As to her sea-worthiness even Tom could not say, but she looked all right. And to the eyes of the members of Ruth Fielding's party there was no threat of bad weather. So why worry about the pleasure-craft's balance and her ability to sail the high seas?

"It is only a short run, anyway," Tom said.

As for Colonel Marchand, he had not the first idea about ships or sailing. He admitted that only continued fair weather and a smooth sea had kept him on deck coming over from France with Jennie and Helen.

At the present time he and Jennie Stone were much too deeply engrossed in each other to think of anything but their own two selves. In a fortnight now, both the Frenchman and Tom would have to return to the battle lines. And they were, deep in their hearts, eager to go back; for they did not dream at this time that the German navy would revolt, that the High Command and the army had lost their morale, and that the end of the Great War was near.

Within Tom's specified hour the party got under way, boarding the *Stazy* from a small boat that came to the camp dock for them. It was not until the yacht was gone with Ruth Fielding and her party that Mr. Hammond set on foot the investigation he had determined upon the night before.

The president of the Alectrion Film Corporation thought a great deal of the girl of the Red Mill. Their friendship was based on something more than a business association. But he knew, too, that after her recent experiences in France and elsewhere, her health was in rather a precarious state.

At least, he was quite sure that Ruth's nerves were "all out of tune," as he expressed it, and he believed she was not entirely responsible for what she had said.

The girl had allowed her mind to dwell so much upon that scenario she had lost that it might be she was not altogether clear upon the subject. Mr. Hammond had talked with Tom about the robbery at the Red Mill, and it looked to the moving picture producer as though there might be some considerable doubt of Ruth's having been robbed at all.

In that terrific wind and rain storm almost anything might have blown away. Tom admitted he had seen a barrel sailing through the air at the height of the storm.

"Why couldn't the papers and note books have been caught up by a gust of wind and carried into the river?" Mr. Hammond asked himself. "The river was right there, and it possesses a strong current."

The president of the Alectrion Film Corporation knew the Lumano, and the vicinity of the Red Mill as well. It seemed to him very probable that the scenario had been lost. And the gold-mounted fountain pen? Why, that might have easily rolled down a crack in the summer-house floor.

The whole thing was a matter so fortuitous that Mr. Hammond could not accept Ruth's version of the loss without some doubt, in any case. And then, her suddenly finding in the only good scenario submitted to him by any of his company, one that she believed was plagiarized from her lost story, seemed to put a cap on the whole matter. Ruth might be just a little "off soundings," as the fishermen about Herringport would say. Mr. Hammond was afraid that she had been carried into a situation of mind where suspicion took the place of certainty.

She had absolutely nothing with which to corroborate her statement. Nobody had seen Ruth's scenario nor had she discussed the plot with any person. Secrecy necessary to the successful production of anything new in the line of picture plays was all right. Mr. Hammond advised it. But in this case it seemed that the scenario writer had been altogether too secret.

Had Ruth not chanced to read the hermit's script before making her accusation, Mr. Hammond would have felt differently. Better, had she been willing to relate to him in the first place the story of the plot of her scenario and how she had treated it, her present accusation might have seemed more reasonable.

But, having read the really good story scrawled on the scraps of brown paper that John, the hermit, had put in the manager's hands, the girl had suddenly claimed the author-ship of the story. There was nothing to prove her claim. It looked dubious at the best.

John, the hermit, was a grim old man. No matter whether he was some old actor hiding away here on Beach Plum Point

Alice B. Emerson

or not, he was not a man to give up easily anything that he had once said was his.

The manager was far too wise to accuse the hermit openly, as Ruth had accused him. They would not get far with the old fellow that way, he was sure.

First of all he called the company together and asked if there were any more scenarios to be submitted. "No," being the answer, he told them briefly that out of the twenty-odd stories he had accepted one that might be whipped into shape for filming—and one only.

Each story submitted had been numbered and the number given to its author. The scripts could now be obtained by the presentation of the numbers. He did not tell them which number had proved successful. Nor did he let it be known that he proposed to try to film the hermit's production.

Mr. Hooley was using old John on this day in a character part. For these "types" the director usually paid ten or fifteen dollars a day; but John was so successful in every part he was given that Mr. Hooley always paid him an extra five dollars for his work. Money seemed to make no difference in the hermit's appearance, however. He wore just as shabby clothing and lived just as plainly as he had when the picture company had come on to the lot.

When work was over for the day, Hooley sent the old man to Mr. Hammond's office. The president of the company invited the hermit into his shack and gave him a seat. He scrutinized the man sharply as he thus greeted him. It was quite true that the hermit did not wholly fit the character he assumed as a longshore waif.

In the first place, his skin was not tanned to the proper

leathery look. His eyes were not those of a man used to looking off over the sea. His hands were too soft and unscarred for a sailor's. He had never pulled on ropes and handled an oar!

Now that Ruth Fielding had suggested that his character was a disguise, Mr. Hammond saw plainly that she must be right. As he was a good actor of other parts before the camera, so he was a good actor in his part of "hermit."

"How long have you lived over there on the point, John?" asked Mr. Hammond carelessly.

"A good many years, sir, in summer."

"How did you come to live there first?"

"I wandered down this way, found the hut empty, turned to and fixed it up, and stayed on."

He said it quite simply and without the first show of confusion. But this tale of his occupancy of the seaside hut he had repeated frequently, as Mr. Hammond very well knew.

"Where do you go in the winter, John?" the latter asked.

"To where it's a sight warmer. I don't have to ask anybody where I shall go," and now the man's tone was a trifle defiant.

"I would like to know something more about you," Mr. Hammond said, quite frankly. "I may be able to do something with your story. We like to know about the person who submits a scenario—"

"That don't go!" snapped the hermit grimly. "You offered

five hundred for a story you could use. If you can use mine, I want the five hundred. And I don't aim to give you the history of my past along with the story. It's nobody's business what or who I am, or where I came from, or where I am going."

"Hoity-toity!" exclaimed Mr. Hammond. "You are quite sudden, aren't you? Now, just calm yourself. I haven't got to take your scenario and pay you five hundred dollars for it—"

"Then somebody else will," said the hermit, getting up.

"Ah! You are quite sure you have a good story here, are you?"

"I know I have."

"And how do you know so much?" sharply demanded the moving picture magnate.

"I've seen enough of this thing you are doing, now—this 'Seaside Idyl' stuff—to know that mine is a hundred per cent. better," sneered the hermit.

"Whew! You've a good opinion of your story, haven't you?" asked Mr. Hammond. "Did you ever write a scenario before?"

"What is that to you?" returned the other. "I don't get you at all, Mr. Hammond. All this cross-examination—"

"That will do now!" snapped the manager. "I am not obliged to take your story. You can try it elsewhere if you like," and he shoved the newspaper-wrapped package toward the end of his desk and nearer the hermit's hand. "I tell you frankly that I won't take any story without knowing all about the author. There are too many comebacks in this game."

"What do you mean?" demanded the other stiffly.

"I don't *know* that your story is original. Frankly, I have some doubt about that very point."

The old man did not change color at all. His gray eyes blazed and he was not at all pleasant looking. But the accusation did not seem to surprise him.

"Are you trying to get it away from me for less than you offered?" he demanded.

"You are an old man," said Mr. Hammond hotly, "and that lets you get away with such a suggestion as that without punishment. I begin to believe that there is something dead wrong with you, John—or whatever your name is."

He drew back the packet of manuscript, opened a drawer, put it within, and locked the drawer.

"I'll think this over a little longer," he said grimly. "At least, until you are willing to be a little more communicative about yourself. I would be glad to use your story with some fixing up, if I was convinced you really wrote it all. But you have got to show me—or give me proper references."

"Give me back the scenario, then!" exclaimed the old man, his eyes blazing hotly.

"No. Not yet. I can take my time in deciding upon the manuscripts submitted in this contest. You will have to wait until I decide," said Mr. Hammond, waving the man out of his office.

# CHAPTER XXI

## A HERMIT FOR REVENUE ONLY

The bays and inlets of the coast of Maine have the bluest water dotted by the greenest islands that one can imagine. And such wild and romantic looking spots as some of these islands are!

Just at this time, too, a particular tang of romance was in the air. The Germans had threatened to devastate our Atlantic coast from Eastport to Key West with a flock of submersibles. There actually were a few submarines lurking about the pathways of our coastwise shipping; but, as usual, the Hun's boast came to naught.

The young people on the *Stazy* scarcely expected to see a German periscope during the run to Reef Harbor. Yet they did not neglect watching out for something of the kind. Skipper Phil Gordon, a young man with one arm but a full and complete knowledge of this coast and how to coax speed out of a gasoline engine, ordered his "crew" of one boy to remain sharply on the lookout, as well.

The *Stazy* did not, however, run far outside. The high and rocky headland that marked the entrance to Reef Harbor came into view before they had more than dropped the hazy outline of Beach Plum Point astern.

But until they rounded the promontory and entered the narrow inlet to Reef Harbor the town and the summer colony was entirely invisible.

"If a German sub should stick its nose in here," sighed Helen, "it would make everybody ashore get up and dust. Don't you think so?"

"Is it the custom to do so when the enemy, he arrive?" asked Colonel Marchand, to whom the idiomatic speech of the Yankee was still a puzzle.

"Sure!" replied Tom, grinning. "Sure, Henri! These New England women would clean house, no matter what catastrophe arrived."

"Oh, don't suggest such horrid possibilities," cried Jennie. "And they are only fooling you, Henri."

"Look yonder!" exclaimed Captain Tom, waving an instructive hand. "Behold! Let the Kaiser's underseas boat come. That little tin lizzie of the sea is ready for it. Depth bombs and all!"

The grim looking drab submarine chaser lay at the nearest dock, the faint spiral of smoke rising from her stack proclaiming that she was ready for immediate work. There was a tower, too, on the highest point on the headland from which a continual watch was kept above the town.

"O-o-oh!" gurgled Jennie, snuggling up to Henri. "Suppose one of those German subs shelled the movie camp back there on Beach Plum Point!"

"They would likely spoil a perfectly good picture, then," said Helen practically. "Think of Ruthie's 'Seaside Idyl!'.

"Oh, say!" Helen went on. "They tell me that old hermit has submitted a story in the contest. What do you suppose it is like, Ruth?"

The girl of the Red Mill was sitting beside Aunt Kate. She flushed when she said:

"Why shouldn't he submit one?"

"But that hermit isn't quite right in his head, is he?" demanded Ruth's chum.

"I don't know that it is his head that is wrong," murmured Ruth, shaking her own head doubtfully.

Here Jennie broke in. "Is auntie letting you read her story, Ruth?" she asked slyly.

"Now, Jennie Stone!" exclaimed their chaperon, blushing.

"Well, you are writing one. You know you are," laughed her niece.

"I—I am just trying to see if I can write such a story," stammered Aunt Kate.

"Well, I am sure you could make up a better scenario than that old grouch of a hermit," Helen declared, warmly.

Ruth did not add anything to this discussion. What she had discovered regarding the hermit's scenario was of too serious a nature to be publicly discussed.

Her interview the evening before with Mr. Hammond regarding the matter had left Ruth in a most uncertain frame of mind. She did not know what to do about the stolen scenario. She shrank from telling even Helen or Tom of her discovery.

To tell the truth, Mr. Hammond's seeming doubt—not of her truthfulness but of her wisdom—had shaken the girl's belief in herself. It was a strange situation, indeed. She thought of the woman she had found wandering about the mountain in the storm who had lost control of both her nerves and her mind, and Ruth wondered if it could be possible that she, too, was on the verge of becoming a nervous wreck.

Had she deceived herself about this hermit's story? Had she allowed her mind to dwell on her loss until she was quite unaccountable for her mental decisions? To tell the truth, this thought frightened the girl of the Red Mill a little.

Practical as Ruth Fielding ordinarily was, she must confess that the shock she had received when the hospital in France was partly wrecked, an account of which is given in "Ruth Fielding Homeward Bound," had shaken the very foundations of her being. She shuddered even now when she thought of what she had been through in France and on the voyage coming back to America.

She realized that even Tom and Helen looked at her sometimes when she spoke of her lost scenario in a most peculiar way. Was it a fact that she had allowed her loss to unbalance —well, her judgment? Suppose she was quite wrong about that scenario the hermit had submitted to Mr. Hammond? The thought frightened her!

At least, she had nothing to say upon the puzzling subject, not even to her best and closest friends. She was sorry indeed two hours later when they were at lunch on the porch of the

Reef Harbor House with some of the Camerons' friends that Helen brought the conversation around again to the Beach Plum Point "hermit."

"A *real* hermit?" cried Cora Grimsby, a gay, blonde, irresponsible little thing, but with a heart of gold. "And is he a hermit for revenue only, too?"

"What do you mean by that?" Helen demanded.

"Why, we have a hermit here, you see. Over on Reef Island itself. If you give us a sail in your motor yacht after lunch I'll introduce our hermit to you. But you must buy something of him, or otherwise 'cross his palm with silver.' He told me one day that he was not playing a nut for summer folks to laugh at just for the good of his health."

"Frank, I must say," laughed Tom Cameron.

"I guess he's been in the hermit business before," said Cora, sparkling at Tom in his uniform. "But this is his first season at the Harbor."

"I wonder if he belongs to the hermit's union and carries a union card," suggested Jennie Stone soberly. "I don't think we should patronize non-union hermits."

"Goody!" cried Cora, clapping her hands. "Let's ask him."

Ruth said nothing. She rather wished she might get out of the trip to Reef Island without offending anybody. But that seemed impossible. She really had seen all the hermits she cared to see!

She could not, however, be morose and absent-minded in a party of which Cora Grimsby and Jennie Stone were the moving spirits. It was a gay crowd that crossed the harbor in the *Stazy* to land at a roughly built dock under the high bluff of the wooded island.

"There's the hermit!" Cora cried, as they landed. "See him sitting on the rock before the door of his cabin?"

"Right on the job," suggested Tom.

"No unlucky city fly shall escape that spider's web," cried Jennie.

He was a patriarchal looking man. His beard swept his breast. He wore shabby garments, was barefooted, and carried a staff as though he were lame or rheumatic.

"Dresses the part much better than our hermit does," Helen said, in comment.

The man met the party from the *Stazy* with a broad smile that displayed a toothless cavity of a mouth. His red-rimmed eyes were moist looking, not to say bleary. Ruth smelled a distinct alcoholic odor on his breath. A complete drouth had evidently not struck this part of the State of Maine.

"Good day to ye!" said the hermit. "Some o' you young folks I ain't never seed before."

"They are my friends," Cora hastened to explain, "and they come from Beach Plum Point."

"Do tell! If you air goin' back to-night, better make a good v'y'ge of it. We're due for a blow, I allow. You folks ain't stoppin' right on the p'int, be ye?"

Ruth, to whom he addressed this last question, answered that they were, and explained that there was a large camp there this season, and why.

"Wal, wal! I want to know! Somebody did say something to me about a gang of movin' picture folks comin' there; but I reckoned they was a-foolin' me."

"There is a good sized party of us," acknowledged Ruth.

"Wal, wal! Mebbe that fella I let my shack to will make out well, then, after all. Warn't no sign of ye on the beach when I left three weeks ago".

"Did you live there on the point?" asked Ruth.

"Allus do winters. But the pickin's is better over here at the Harbor at this time of year."

"And the man you left in your place? Where is your house on the point?"

The hermit "for revenue only" described the hut on the eastern shore in which the other "hermit" lived. Ruth became much interested.

"Tell me," she said, while the others examined the curios the hermit had for sale, "what kind of man is this you left in your house? And who is he?"

"Law bless ye!" said the old man. "I don't know him from Adam's off ox. Never seed him afore. But he was trampin' of it; and he didn't have much money. An' to tell you the truth, Miss, that hutch of mine ain't wuth much money."

She described the man who had been playing the hermit since the Alectrion Film Corporation crowd had come to

Beach Plum Point.

"That's the fella," said the old man, nodding.

Ruth stood aside while he waited on his customers and digested these statements regarding the man who claimed the authorship of the scenario of "Plain Mary."

Not that Ruth would have desired to acknowledge the scenario in its present form. She felt angry every time she thought of how her plot had been mangled.

But she was glad to learn all that was known about the Beach Plum Point hermit. And she had learned one most important fact.

He was not a regular hermit. As Jennie Stone suggested, he was not a "union hermit" at all. And he was a stranger to the neighborhood of Herringport. If he had been at the Point only three weeks, as this old man said, "John, the hermit," might easily have come since Ruth's scenario was stolen back there at the Red Mill!

Her thoughts began to mill again about this possibility. She wished she was back at the camp so as to put the strange old man through a cross-examination regarding himself and where he had come from. She had no suspicion as to how Mr. Hammond had so signally failed in this very matter.

Alice B. Emerson

# CHAPTER XXII

## AN ARRIVAL

Mr. Hammond was in no placid state of mind himself after the peculiarly acting individual who called himself "John, the hermit," left his office. The very fact that the man refused to tell anything about his personal affairs—who he really was, or where he came from—induced the moving picture producer to believe there must be something wrong about him.

Mr. Hammond went to the door of the shack and watched the man tramping up the beach toward the end of the point. What a dignified stride he had! Rather, it was the stride of a poseur—like nothing so much as that of the old-time tragedian, made famous by the Henry Irving school of actors.

"An ancient 'ham' sure enough, just as the boys say," muttered the manager.

The so-called hermit disappeared. The moving picture people were gathering for dinner. The sun, although still above the horizon, was dimmed by cloud-banks which were rising steadily to meet clouds over the sea.

A wan light played upon the heaving "graybacks" outside the

mouth of the harbor. The wind whined among the pines which grew along the ridge of Beach Plum Point.

A storm was imminent. Just as Mr. Hammond took note of this and wished that Ruth Fielding and her party had returned, a snorting automobile rattled along the shell road and halted near the camp.

"Is this the Alectrion Film Company?" asked a shrill voice.

"This is the place, Miss," said the driver of the small car.

The chauffeur ran his jitney from the railroad station and was known to Mr. Hammond. The latter went nearer.

Out of the car stepped a girl—a very young girl to be traveling alone. She was dressed in extreme fashion, but very cheaply. Her hair was bobbed and she wore a Russian blouse of cheap silk. Her skirt was very narrow, her cloth boots very high, and the heels of them were like those of Jananese clogs.

What with the skimpy skirt and the high heels she could scarcely walk. She was laden with two bags—one an ancient carpet-bag that must have been seventy-five years old, and the other a bright tan one of imitation leather with brass clasps. She wore a coal-scuttle hat pulled down over her eyes so that her face was quite extinguished.

Altogether her get-up was rather startling. Mr. Hammond saw Jim Hooley come out of his tent to stare at the new arrival. She certainly was a "type."

There was a certain kind of prettiness about the girl, and aside from her incongruous garments she was not unattractive—when her face was revealed. Mr. Hammond's interest

Alice B. Emerson

increased. He approached the spot where the girl had been left by the jitney driver.

"You came to see somebody?" he asked kindly. "Who is it you wish to see?"

"Is this the moving picture camp, Mister?" she returned.

"Yes," said the manager, smiling. "Are you acquainted with somebody who works here?"

"Yes. I am Arabella Montague Fitzmaurice," said the girl, with an air that seemed to show that she expected to be recognized when she had recited her name.

Mr. Hammond refrained from open laughter. He only said:

"Why—that is nice. I am glad to meet you, my dear. Who are you looking for?"

"I want to see my pa, of course. I guess you know who *he* is?"

"I am not sure that I do, my dear."

"You don't—Say! who are you?" demanded Bella, with some sharpness.

"I am only the manager of the company. Who is your father, child?"

"Well, of all the—Wouldn't that give you your never-gitovers!" exclaimed Bella, in broad amazement. "Say! I guess my pa is your leading man."

"Mr. Hasbrouck? Impossible!"

"Never heard of him," said Bella, promptly. "Montague Fitzmaurice, I mean."

"And I never heard of him," declared Mr. Hammond, both puzzled and amused.

"What?" gasped the girl, almost stunned by this statement. "Maybe you know him as Mr. Pike. That is our honest-to-goodness name—Pike."

"I am sorry that you are disappointed, my dear," said the manager kindly. "But don't be worried. If you expected to meet your father here, perhaps he will come later. But really, I have no such person as that on my staff at the present time."

"I don't know—Why!" cried Bella, "he sent me money and said he was working here. I—I didn't tell him I was coming. I just got sick of those Perkinses, and I took the money and went to Boston and got dressed up, and then came on here. I—I just about spent all the money he sent me to get here."

"Well, that was perhaps unwise," said Mr. Hammond. "But don't worry. Come along now to Mother Paisley. She will look out for you—and you can stay with us until your father appears. There is some mistake somewhere."

By this speech he warded off tears. Bella hastily winked them back and squared her thin shoulders.

"All right, sir," she said, picking up the bags again. "Pa will make it all right with you. He wrote in his letter as if he had a good engagement."

Mr. Hammond might have learned something further about this surprising girl at the time, but just as he introduced her to Mother Paisley one of the men came running from the point and hailed him:

"Mr. Hammond! There's a boat in trouble off the point. I think she was making for this harbor. Have you got a pair of glasses?"

Mr. Hammond had a fine pair of opera glasses, and he produced them from his desk while he asked:

"What kind of boat is it, Maxwell?"

"Looks like that blue motor that Miss Fielding and her friends went off in this morning. We saw it coming along at top speed. And suddenly it stopped. They can't seem to manage it—"

The manager hurried with Maxwell along the sands. The sky was completely overcast now, and the wind whipped the spray from the wave tops into their faces. The weather looked dubious indeed, and the manager of the film corporation was worried before even he focused his glasses upon the distant motor-boat.

# CHAPTER XXIII

## TROUBLE—PLENTY

Even Ruth Fielding had paid no attention to the warning of the Reef Island hermit regarding a change in the weather, in spite of the fact that she was anxious to return to the camp near Herringport. It was not until the *Stazy* was outside the inlet late in the afternoon that Skipper Phil Gordon noted the threatening signs in sea and sky.

"That's how it goes," the one-armed mariner said. "When we aren't dependent on the wind to fill our canvas, we neglect watching every little weather change. She's going to blow by and by."

"Do you think it will be a real storm?" asked Ruth, who sat beside him at the steering wheel and engine, watching how he managed the mechanism.

"Maybe. But with good luck we will make Beach Plum Point long before it amounts to anything."

The long graybacks were rather pleasant to ride over at first. Even Aunt Kate was not troubled by the prospect. It was so short a run to the anchorage behind the Point that nobody expressed fear.

Alice B. Emerson

When the spray began to fly over the bows the girls merely squealed a bit, although they hastily found extra wraps. If the *Stazy* plunged and shipped half a sea now and then, nobody was made anxious. And soon the Point was in plain view.

To make the run easier, however, Skipper Gordon had sailed the motor-yacht well out to sea. When he shifted the helm to run for the entrance to the bay, the waves began to slap against the *Stazy's* side. She rolled terrifically and the aspect of affairs was instantly changed.

"Oh, dear me!" moaned Jennie Stone. "How do you feel, Henri? I did not bargain for this rough stuff, did you? Oh!"

"'Mister Captain, stop the ship, I want to get off and walk!'" sang Helen gaily. "Don't lose all hope, Heavy. You'll never sink if you do go overboard."

"Isn't she mean?" sniffed the plump girl. "And I am only afraid for Henri's sake."

"I don't like this for my own sake," murmured Aunt Kate.

"Are you cold, dear?" her niece asked, with quick sympathy. "Here! I don't really need this cape with my heavy sweater."

She removed the heavy cloth garment from her own shoulders and with a flirt sought to place it around Aunt Kate. The wind swooped down just then with sudden force. The *Stazy* rolled to leeward.

"Oh! Stop it!"

Bulging under pressure of the wind, the cape flew over the rail. Jennie tried to clutch it again; Henri plunged after it, too. Colliding, the two managed between them to miss the garment altogether. It dropped into the water just under the rail.

"Of all the clumsy fingers!" ejaculated Helen. But she could not seize the wrap, although she darted for it. Nor could Ruth help, she being still farther forward.

"Now, you've done it!" complained Aunt Kate.

The boat began to rise on another roller. The cape was sucked out of sight under the rail. The next moment the whirling propeller was stopped—so abruptly that the *Stazy* shook all over.

"Oh! what has happened?" shrieked Helen.

Ruth started up, and Tom seized her arm to steady her. But the girl of the Red Mill did not express any fear. The shock did not seem to affect her so much as it did the other girls. Here was a real danger, and Ruth did not lose her self-possession.

Phil Gordon had shut off the power, and the motor-boat began to swing broadside to the rising seas.

"The propeller is broken!" cried Tom.

"She's jammed. That cape!" gasped the one-armed skipper. "Here! Tend to this till I see what can be done. Jack!" he shouted to his crew. "This way—lively, now!"

But Ruth slipped into his place before Tom could do so.

"I know how to steer, Tommy," she declared. "And I under-stand the engine. Give him a hand if he needs you."

"Oh, we'll turn turtle!" shrieked Jennie, as the boat rolled again.

"You'll never become a turtle, Jen," declared Tom, plunging aft. "Turtles are dumb!"

The *Stazy* was slapped by a big wave, "just abaft the starboard bow," to be real nautical, and half a ton of seawater washed over the forward deck and spilled into the standing-room of the craft.

Henri had wisely closed the door of the cabin. The water foamed about their feet. Ruth found herself knee deep for a moment in this flood. She whirled the wheel over, trying to bring up the head of the craft to meet the next wave.

"Oh, my dear!" groaned Jennie Stone. "We are going to be drowned."

"Drowned, your granny!" snapped Helen angrily. "Don't be such a silly, Jennie."

Ruth stood at the wheel with more apparent calmness than any of them. Her hair had whipped out of its fastenings and streamed over her shoulders. Her eyes were bright and her cheeks aglow.

Helen, staring at her, suddenly realized that this was the old Ruth Fielding. Her chum had not looked so much alive, so thoroughly competent and ready for anything, before for weeks.

"Why—why, Ruthie!" Helen murmured, "I believe you like this."

Her chum did not hear the words, but she suddenly flashed

Helen a brilliant smile. "Keep up your pluck, child!" she shouted. "We'll come out all right."

Again the *Stazy* staggered under the side swipe of a big wave.

"Ye-ow!" yelped Tom in the stern, almost diving overboard.

"Steady!" shouted Skipper Gordon, excitedly.

"Steady she is, Captain!" rejoined Ruth Fielding, and actually laughed.

"How can you, Ruth?" complained Jennie, clinging to Henri Marchand. "And when we are about to drown."

"Weeping will not save us," flung back Ruth.

Her strong hands held the wheel-spokes with a grip unbreakable. She could force the *Stazy's* head to the seas.

"Can you start the engine on the reverse, Miss?" bawled Gordon.

"I can try!" flashed Ruth. "Say when."

In a moment the cry came: "Ready!"

"Aye, aye!" responded Ruth, spinning the flywheel.

The spark caught almost instantly. The exhaust sputtered.

"Now!" yelled the skipper.

Ruth threw the lever. The boat trembled like an automobile under the propulsion of the engine. The propeller

Alice B. Emerson

shaft groaned.

"Ye-ow!" shouted the excited Tom again.

This time he sprawled back into the bottom of the boat, tearing away a good half of Jennie's cape in his grip. The rest of the garment floated to the surface. It was loose from the propeller.

"Full speed ahead!" shouted the one-armed captain of the motor-boat.

Ruth obeyed the command. The *Stazy* staggered into the next wave. The water that came in over her bow almost drowned them, but Ruth, hanging to the steering wheel, brought the craft through the roller without swamping her.

"Good for our Ruth!" shouted Helen, as soon as she could get her breath.

"Oh, Ruth! you always come to our rescue," declared Jennie gratefully.

"Hi! I thought you were a nervous wreck, young lady," Tom sputtered, scrambling forward to relieve her. "Get you into a tight corner, and you show what you are made of, all right."

The girl of the Red Mill smiled at them. She had done something! Nor did she feel at all overcome by the effort. The danger through which they had passed had inspired rather than frightened her.

"Why, I'm all right," she told Tom when he reached her. "This is great! We'll be behind the shelter of the Point in a few minutes. There's nothing to worry about."

"You're all right, Ruth," Tom repeated, admiringly. "I thought you'd lost your grip, but I see you haven't. You are the same old Ruthie Fielding, after all."

# CHAPTER XXIV

## ABOUT "PLAIN MARY"

Mr. Hammond and the actors with him had no idea of the nature of the accident that had happened to the *Stazy*. From the extreme end of Beach Plum Point they could merely watch proceedings aboard the craft, and wonder what it was all about.

The manager could, however, see through his glasses that Ruth Fielding was at the wheel. Her face came out clear as a cameo when he focused the opera glasses upon her. And at the change in the girl's expression he marveled.

Those ashore could do nothing to aid the party on the motor-yacht; and until it got under way again Mr. Hammond was acutely anxious. It rolled so that he expected it to turn keel up at almost any moment.

Before the blasts of rain began to sweep across the sea, however, the *Stazy* was once more under control. At that most of the spectators made for the camp and shelter. But the manager of the film corporation waited to see the motor-yacht inside the shelter of Beach Plum Point.

The rain was falling heavily, and not merely in gusts, when

Ruth and her friends came ashore in the small boat. The lamps were lit and dinner was over at the main camp. Therefore the automobile touring party failed to see Bella Pike or hear about her arrival. By this time the girl had gone off to the main dormitory with Mother Paisley, and even Mr. Hammond did not think of her.

Nor did the manager speak that evening to Ruth about the hermit's scenario or his interview with the old man regarding it.

The three girls and Aunt Kate changed their clothing in the little shack and then joined the young men in the dining room for a late supper. Aunt Kate was to stay this night at the camp. There was a feeling of much thankfulness in all their hearts over their escape from what might have been a serious accident.

"Providence was good to us," said Aunt Kate. "I hope we are all properly grateful."

"And properly proud of Ruthie!" exclaimed Helen, squeezing her chum's hand.

"Don't throw too many bouquets," laughed Ruth. "It was not I that tore Jennie's cape out of the propeller. I merely obeyed the skipper's orders."

"She is a regular Cheerful Grig again, isn't she?" demanded Jennie, beaming on Ruth.

"I have been a wet blanket on this party long enough. I just begin to realize how very unpleasant I have been—"

"Not that, Mademoiselle!" objected Henri.

"But yes! Hereafter I will be cheerful. Life is worth living after all!"

Tom, who sat next to her at table (he usually managed to do that) smiled at Ruth approvingly.

"Bravo!" he whispered. "There are other scenarios to write."

"Tom!" she whispered sharply, "I want to tell you something about that."

"About what?"

"My scenario."

"You don't mean—"

"I mean I know what has become of it."

"Never!" gasped Tom. "Are you—are—you—"

"I am not '*non compos*,' and-so-forth," laughed Ruth. "Oh, there is nothing foolish about this, Tom. Let me tell you."

She spoke in so low a tone that the others could not have heard had they desired to. She and Tom put their heads together and within the next few minutes Ruth had told him all about the hermit's scenario and her conviction that he had stolen his idea and a large part of his story from Ruth's lost manuscript.

"It seems almost impossible, Ruth," gasped her friend.

"No. Not impossible or improbable. Listen to what that man on Reef Island told me about this hermit, so-called." And she repeated it all to the excited Tom. "I am convinced," pursued

Ruth, "that this hermit could easily have been in the vicinity of the Red Mill on the day my manuscript disappeared."

"But to prove it!" cried Tom.

"We'll see about that," said Ruth confidently. "You know, Ben told us he had seen and spoken to a tramp-actor that day. Uncle Jabez saw him, too. And you, Tom, followed his trail to the Cheslow railroad yards."

"So I did," admitted her friend.

"I believe," went on Ruth earnestly, "that this man who came here to live on Beach Plum Point only three weeks ago, is that very vagrant. It is plain that this fellow is playing the part of a hermit, just as he plays the parts Mr. Hooley casts him for."

"Whew!" whistled Tom. "Almost do you convince me, Ruth Fielding. But to prove it is another thing."

"We *will* prove it. If this man was at the Red Mill on that particular day, we can make sure of the fact."

"How will you do it, Ruth?"

"By getting one of the camera men to take a 'still' of the hermit, develop it for us, and send the negative to Ben. He and Uncle Jabez must remember how that traveling actor looked—"

"Hurrah!" exclaimed Tom, jumping up to the amazement of the rest of the party. "That's a bully idea."

"What is it?" demanded Helen. "Let us in on it, too."

But Ruth shook her head and Tom calmed down.

"Can't tell the secret yet," Helen's twin declared. "That would spoil it."

"Oh! A surprise! I love surprises," said Jennie Stone.

"I don't. Not when my chum and my brother have a secret from me and won't let me in on it," and Helen turned her back upon them in apparent indignation.

After that Ruth and Tom discussed the matter with more secrecy. Ruth said in conclusion:

"If he was there at the mill the day my story was stolen, and now submits this scenario to Mr. Hammond—and it is merely a re-hash of mine, Tom, I assure you—"

"Of course I believe you, Ruth," rejoined the young fellow.

"Mr. Hammond should be convinced, too," said the girl.

But there was a point that Tom saw very clearly and which Ruth Fielding did not seem to appreciate. She still had no evidence to corroborate her claim that the hermit's story of "Plain Mary" was plagiarized from her manuscript.

For, after all, nobody but Ruth herself knew what her scenario had been like!

# CHAPTER XXV

## LIFTING THE CURTAIN

Ruth slept peacefully and awoke the next morning in a perfectly serene frame of mind. She was quite as convinced as ever that she had been robbed of her scenario; and she was, as well, sure that "John, the hermit," had produced his picture play from her manuscript. But Ruth no longer felt anxious and excited about it.

She clearly saw her way to a conclusion of the matter. If the old actor was identified by Ben and Uncle Jabez as the tramp they had seen and conversed with, the girl of the Red Mill was pretty sure she would get the best of the thief.

In the first place she considered her idea and her scenario worth much more than five hundred dollars. If by no other means, she would buy the hermit's story at the price Mr. Hammond was willing to pay for it—and a little more if necessary. And if possible she would force the old actor to hand over to her the script that she had lost.

Thus was her mind made up, and she approached the matter in all cheerfulness. She had said nothing to anybody but Tom, and she did not see him early in the morning. One of the stewards brought the girls' breakfast to the shack; so they

Alice B. Emerson

knew little of what went on about the camp at that time.

The rain had ceased. The storm had passed on completely. Soon after breakfast Ruth saw the man who called himself "John, the hermit," making straight for Mr. Hammond's office.

That was where Ruth wished to be. She wanted to confront the man before the president of the film corporation. She started over that way and ran into the most surprising incident!

Coming out of the cook tent with a huge apron enveloping her queer, tight dress and tilting forward upon her high heels, appeared Bella Pike! Ruth Fielding might have met somebody whose presence here would have surprised her more, but at the moment she could not imagine who it could be.

"Ara-bella!" gasped Ruth.

The child turned to stare her own amazement. She changed color, too, for she knew she had done wrong to run away; but she smiled with both eyes and lips, for she was glad to see Ruth.

"My mercy!" she ejaculated. "If it ain't Miss Fielding! How-do, Miss Fielding? Ain't it enough to give one their nevergitovers to see you here?"

"And how do you suppose I feel to find you here at Beach Plum Point," demanded Ruth, "when we all thought you were so nicely fixed with Mr. and Mrs. Perkins? And Mrs. Holmes wrote to me only the other day that you seemed contented."

"That's right, Miss Fielding," sighed the actor's child. "I was. And Miz Perkins was always nice to me. Nothing at all like Aunt Suse Timmins. But, you see, they ain't like pa."

"Did your father bring you here?"

"No'm."

"Nor send for you?"

"Not exactly," confessed Bella.

"Well!"

"You see, he sent me money. Only on Tuesday. Forty dollars."

"Forty dollars! And to a child like you?"

"Well, Miss Fielding, if he had sent it to Aunt Suse I'd never have seen a penny of it. And pa didn't know what you'd done for me and how you'd put me with Miz Perkins."

"I suppose that is so," admitted the surprised Ruth. "But why did you come here?"

"'Cause pa wrote he had an engagement here. I came through Boston, an' got me a dress, and some shoes, and a hat—all up to date—and I thought I'd surprise pa—"

"But, Bella! I haven't seen your father here, have I?"

"No. There's a mistake somehow. But this nice Miz Paisley says for me not to worry. That like enough pa will come here yet."

"I never!" ejaculated Ruth. "Come right along with me, Bella, and see Mr. Hammond. Something must be done. Of course, Mrs. Perkins and the doctor's wife have no idea where you have gone?"

"Oh, yes'm. I left a note telling 'em I'd gone to meet pa."

"But we must send them a message that you are all right. Come on, Bella!" and with her arm about the child's thin shoulders, Ruth urged her to Mr. Hammond's office—and directly into her father's arms!

This was how Arabella Montague Fitzmaurice Pike came to meet her father—in a most amazing fashion!

"Pa! I never did!" half shrieked the queer child.

"Arabella! Here? How strange!" observed the man who had been acting the part of the Beach Plum Point hermit. "My child!"

Mr. Pike could do nothing save in a dramatic way. He seized Bella and hugged her to his bosom in a most stagy manner. But Ruth saw that the man's gray eyes were moist, that his hands when he seized the girl really trembled, and he kissed Bella with warmth.

"I declare!" exclaimed Mr. Hammond. "So your name is something-or-other-Fitzmaurice Pike?"

"John Pike, if it please you. The other is for professional purposes only," said Bella's father. "If you do not mind, sir," he added, "we will postpone our discussion until a later time. I—I would take my daughter to my poor abode and learn of her experience in getting here to Beach Plum Point."

"Go as far as you like, Mr. Pike. But remember there has got to be a settlement later of this matter we were discussing," said the manager sternly.

The actor and his daughter departed, the former giving Ruth a very curious look indeed. Mr. Hammond turned a broad smile upon the girl of the Red Mill.

"What do you know about *that*?" Mr. Hammond demanded. "Why, Miss Ruth, yours seems to have been a very good guess. That fellow is an old-timer and no mistake."

"My guess was good in more ways than one," said Ruth. "I believe I can prove that this Pike was at the Red Mill on the day my scenario was stolen."

She told the manager briefly of the discovery she had made through the patriarchal old fellow on Reef Island the day before, and of her intention of sending a photograph of Pike back home for identification.

"Good idea!" declared Mr. Hammond. "I will speak to Mr. Hooley. There are 'stills' on file of all the people he is using here on the lot at the present time. If you are really sure this man's story is a plagiarism on your own—"

She smiled at him. "I can prove that, too, I think, to your satisfaction. I feel now that I can sit down and roughly sketch my whole scenario again. I must confess that in two places in this 'Plain Mary' this man Pike has really improved on my idea. But as a whole his manuscript does not flatter my story. You'll see!"

"Truly, you are a different young woman this morning, Miss Ruth!" exclaimed her friend. "I hope this matter will be settled in a way satisfactory to you. I really think there is the

Alice B. Emerson

germ of a splendid picture in this 'Plain Mary.'"

"And believe me!" laughed Ruth, "the germ is mine. You'll see," she repeated.

She proved her point, and Mr. Hammond did see; but the outcome was through quite unexpected channels. Ruth did not have to threaten the man who had made her all the trouble. John M. F. Pike made his confession of his own volition when they discussed the matter that very day.

"I feel, Miss Fielding, after all that you did for my child, that I cannot go on with this subterfuge that, for Bella's sake, I was tempted to engage in. I did seize upon your manuscript in that summer-house near the mill where they say you live, and I was prepared to make the best use of it possible for Bella's sake.

"We have had such bad luck! Poverty for one's self is bad enough. I have withstood the slings and arrows of outrageous fortune for years. But my child is growing up—"

"Would you want her to grow up to know that her father is a thief?" Ruth demanded hotly.

"Hunger under the belt gnaws more potently than conscience," said Pike, with a grandiloquent gesture. "I had sought alms and been refused at that mill. Lurking about I saw you leave the summer-house and spied the gold pen. I can give you a pawn ticket for that," said Mr. Pike sadly. "But I saw, too, the value of your scenario and notes. Desperately I had determined to try to enter this field of moving pictures. It is a terrible come down, Miss Fielding, for an artist—this mugging before the camera."

He went on in his roundabout way to tell her that he had no

idea of the ownership of the scenario. Her name was not on it, and he had not observed her face that day at the Red Mill. And in his mind all the time had been his own and his child's misery.

"It was a bold attempt to forge success through dishonesty," he concluded with humility.

Whether Ruth was altogether sure that Pike was quite honest in his confession or not, for Bella's sake she could not be harsh with the old actor. Nor could he, Ruth believed, be wholly bad when he loved his child so much.

As he turned over to Ruth every scrap of manuscript, as well as the notebooks she had lost, she need not worry about establishing her ownership of the script.

When Mr. Hammond had examined her material he agreed with Ruth that in two quite important places Bella's father had considerably improved the original idea of the story.

This gave Ruth the lead she had been looking for. Mr. Hammond admitted that the story was much too fine and too important to be filmed here at this summer camp. He decided to make a great spectacular production of it at the company's main studio later in the fall.

So Ruth proceeded to force Bella's father to accept two hundred dollars in payment for what he had done on the story. As her contract with Mr. Hammond called for a generous royalty, she would make much more out of the scenario than the sum John Pike had hoped to get by selling the stolen idea to Mr. Hammond.

The prospects of Bella and her father were vastly improved, too. His work as a "type" for picture makers would gain him a much better livelihood than he had been able to earn in the legitimate field. And when Ruth and her party left Beach Plum Point camp for home in their automobiles, Bella herself was working in a two-reel comedy that Mr. Hooley was directing.

"Well, thank goodness!" sighed Helen, "Ruth has settled affairs for two more of her 'waifs and strays.' Now don't, I beg, find anybody else to become interested in during our trip back to the Red Mill, Ruthie."

Ruth was sitting beside Tom on the front seat of the big touring car. He looked at her sideways with a whimsical little smile.

"I wish you would turn over a new leaf, Ruthie," he whispered.

"And what is to be on that new leaf?" she asked brightly.

"Just me. Pay a little attention to yours truly. Remember that in a week I shall go aboard the transport again, and then—"

"Oh, Tom!" she murmured, clasping her hands, "I don't want to think of it. If this awful war would only end!"

"It's the only war so far that hasn't ended," he said. "And I have a feeling, anyway, that it may not last long. Henri and I have got to hurry back to finish it up. Leave it to us, Ruth," and he smiled.

But Ruth sighed. "I suppose I shall have to, Tommy-boy," she said. "And do finish it quickly! I do not feel as though I could return to college, or write another scenario, or do a single, solitary thing until peace is declared."

"And *then*?" asked Tom, significantly.

Ruth gave him an understanding smile.


THE END

Alice B. Emerson

# Choose from Thousands of 1stWorldLibrary Classics By

A. M. Barnard
Ada Leverson
Adolphus William Ward
Aesop
Agatha Christie
Alexander Aaronsohn
Alexander Kielland
Alexandre Dumas
Alfred Gatty
Alfred Ollivant
Alice Duer Miller
Alice Turner Curtis
Alice Dunbar
Allen Chapman
Alleyne Ireland
Ambrose Bierce
Amelia E. Barr
Amory H. Bradford
Andrew Lang
Andrew McFarland Davis
Andy Adams
Angela Brazil
Anna Alice Chapin
Anna Sewell
Annie Besant
Annie Hamilton Donnell
Annie Payson Call
Annie Roe Carr
Annonaymous
Anton Chekhov
Archibald Lee Fletcher
Arnold Bennett
Arthur C. Benson
Arthur Conan Doyle
Arthur M. Winfield
Arthur Ransome
Arthur Schnitzler
Arthur Train
Atticus
B.H. Baden-Powell
B. M. Bower
B. C. Chatterjee
Baroness Emmuska Orczy
Baroness Orczy
Basil King
Bayard Taylor
Ben Macomber
Bertha Muzzy Bower
Bjornstjerne Bjornson

Booth Tarkington
Boyd Cable
Bram Stoker
C. Collodi
C. E. Orr
C. M. Ingleby
Carolyn Wells
Catherine Parr Traill
Charles A. Eastman
Charles Amory Beach
Charles Dickens
Charles Dudley Warner
Charles Farrar Browne
Charles Ives
Charles Kingsley
Charles Klein
Charles Hanson Towne
Charles Lathrop Pack
Charles Romyn Dake
Charles Whibley
Charles Willing Beale
Charlotte M. Braeme
Charlotte M. Yonge
Charlotte Perkins Stetson
Clair W. Hayes
Clarence Day Jr.
Clarence E. Mulford
Clemence Housman
Confucius
Coningsby Dawson
Cornelis DeWitt Wilcox
Cyril Burleigh
D. H. Lawrence
Daniel Defoe
David Garnett
Dinah Craik
Don Carlos Janes
Donald Keyhoe
Dorothy Kilner
Dougan Clark
Douglas Fairbanks
E. Nesbit
E. P. Roe
E. Phillips Oppenheim
E. S. Brooks
Earl Barnes
Edgar Rice Burroughs
Edith Van Dyne
Edith Wharton

Edward Everett Hale
Edward J. O'Biren
Edward S. Ellis
Edwin L. Arnold
Eleanor Atkins
Eleanor Hallowell Abbott
Eliot Gregory
Elizabeth Gaskell
Elizabeth McCracken
Elizabeth Von Arnim
Ellem Key
Emerson Hough
Emilie F. Carlen
Emily Bronte
Emily Dickinson
Enid Bagnold
Enilor Macartney Lane
Erasmus W. Jones
Ernie Howard Pie
Ethel May Dell
Ethel Turner
Ethel Watts Mumford
Eugene Sue
Eugenie Foa
Eugene Wood
Eustace Hale Ball
Evelyn Everett-green
Everard Cotes
F. H. Cheley
F. J. Cross
F. Marion Crawford
Fannie E. Newberry
Federick Austin Ogg
Ferdinand Ossendowski
Fergus Hume
Florence A. Kilpatrick
Fremont B. Deering
Francis Bacon
Francis Darwin
Frances Hodgson Burnett
Frances Parkinson Keyes
Frank Gee Patchin
Frank Harris
Frank Jewett Mather
Frank L. Packard
Frank V. Webster
Frederic Stewart Isham
Frederick Trevor Hill
Frederick Winslow Taylor

Friedrich Kerst
Friedrich Nietzsche
Fyodor Dostoyevsky
G.A. Henty
G.K. Chesterton
Gabrielle E. Jackson
Garrett P. Serviss
Gaston Leroux
George A. Warren
George Ade
Geroge Bernard Shaw
George Cary Eggleston
George Durston
George Ebers
George Eliot
George Gissing
George MacDonald
George Meredith
George Orwell
George Sylvester Viereck
George Tucker
George W. Cable
George Wharton James
Gertrude Atherton
Gordon Casserly
Grace E. King
Grace Gallatin
Grace Greenwood
Grant Allen
Guillermo A. Sherwell
Gulielma Zollinger
Gustav Flaubert
H. A. Cody
H. B. Irving
H. C. Bailey
H. G. Wells
H. H. Munro
H. Irving Hancock
H. R. Naylor
H. Rider Haggard
H. W. C. Davis
Haldeman Julius
Hall Caine
Hamilton Wright Mabie
Hans Christian Andersen
Harold Avery
Harold McGrath
Harriet Beecher Stowe
Harry Castlemon
Harry Coghill
Harry Houidini

Hayden Carruth
Helent Hunt Jackson
Helen Nicolay
Hendrik Conscience
Hendy David Thoreau
Henri Barbusse
Henrik Ibsen
Henry Adams
Henry Ford
Henry Frost
Henry James
Henry Jones Ford
Henry Seton Merriman
Henry W Longfellow
Herbert A. Giles
Herbert Carter
Herbert N. Casson
Herman Hesse
Hildegard G. Frey
Homer
Honore De Balzac
Horace B. Day
Horace Walpole
Horatio Alger Jr.
Howard Pyle
Howard R. Garis
Hugh Lofting
Hugh Walpole
Humphry Ward
Ian Maclaren
Inez Haynes Gillmore
Irving Bacheller
Isabel Cecilia Williams
Isabel Hornibrook
Israel Abrahams
Ivan Turgenev
J. G.Austin
J. Henri Fabre
J. M. Barrie
J. M. Walsh
J. Macdonald Oxley
J. R. Miller
J. S. Fletcher
J. S. Knowles
J. Storer Clouston
J. W. Duffield
Jack London
Jacob Abbott
James Allen
James Andrews
James Baldwin

James Branch Cabell
James DeMille
James Joyce
James Lane Allen
James Lane Allen
James Oliver Curwood
James Oppenheim
James Otis
James R. Driscoll
Jane Abbott
Jane Austen
Jane L. Stewart
Janet Aldridge
Jens Peter Jacobsen
Jerome K. Jerome
Jessie Graham Flower
John Buchan
John Burroughs
John Cournos
John F. Kennedy
John Gay
John Glasworthy
John Habberton
John Joy Bell
John Kendrick Bangs
John Milton
John Philip Sousa
John Taintor Foote
Jonas Lauritz Idemil Lie
Jonathan Swift
Joseph A. Altsheler
Joseph Carey
Joseph Conrad
Joseph E. Badger Jr
Joseph Hergesheimer
Joseph Jacobs
Jules Vernes
Julian Hawthrone
Julie A Lippmann
Justin Huntly McCarthy
Kakuzo Okakura
Karle Wilson Baker
Kate Chopin
Kenneth Grahame
Kenneth McGaffey
Kate Langley Bosher
Kate Langley Bosher
Katherine Cecil Thurston
Katherine Stokes
L. A. Abbot
L. T. Meade

L. Frank Baum
Latta Griswold
Laura Dent Crane
Laura Lee Hope
Laurence Housman
Lawrence Beasley
Leo Tolstoy
Leonid Andreyev
Lewis Carroll
Lewis Sperry Chafer
Lilian Bell
Lloyd Osbourne
Louis Hughes
Louis Joseph Vance
Louis Tracy
Louisa May Alcott
Lucy Fitch Perkins
Lucy Maud Montgomery
Luther Benson
Lydia Miller Middleton
Lyndon Orr
M. Corvus
M. H. Adams
Margaret E. Sangster
Margret Howth
Margaret Vandercook
Margaret W. Hungerford
Margret Penrose
Maria Edgeworth
Maria Thompson Daviess
Mariano Azuela
Marion Polk Angellotti
Mark Overton
Mark Twain
Mary Austin
Mary Catherine Crowley
Mary Cole
Mary Hastings Bradley
Mary Roberts Rinehart
Mary Rowlandson
M. Wollstonecraft Shelley
Maud Lindsay
Max Beerbohm
Myra Kelly
Nathaniel Hawthrone
Nicolo Machiavelli
O. F. Walton
Oscar Wilde
Owen Johnson
P.G. Wodehouse
Paul and Mabel Thorne

Paul G. Tomlinson
Paul Severing
Percy Brebner
Percy Keese Fitzhugh
Peter B. Kyne
Plato
Quincy Allen
R. Derby Holmes
R. L. Stevenson
R. S. Ball
Rabindranath Tagore
Rahul Alvares
Ralph Bonehill
Ralph Henry Barbour
Ralph Victor
Ralph Waldo Emmerson
Rene Descartes
Ray Cummings
Rex Beach
Rex E. Beach
Richard Harding Davis
Richard Jefferies
Richard Le Gallienne
Robert Barr
Robert Frost
Robert Gordon Anderson
Robert L. Drake
Robert Lansing
Robert Lynd
Robert Michael Ballantyne
Robert W. Chambers
Rosa Nouchette Carey
Rudyard Kipling
Saint Augustine
Samuel B. Allison
Samuel Hopkins Adams
Sarah Bernhardt
Sarah C. Hallowell
Selma Lagerlof
Sherwood Anderson
Sigmund Freud
Standish O'Grady
Stanley Weyman
Stella Benson
Stella M. Francis
Stephen Crane
Stewart Edward White
Stijn Streuvels
Swami Abhedananda
Swami Parmananda
T. S. Ackland

T. S. Arthur
The Princess Der Ling
Thomas A. Janvier
Thomas A Kempis
Thomas Anderton
Thomas Bailey Aldrich
Thomas Bulfinch
Thomas De Quincey
Thomas Dixon
Thomas H. Huxley
Thomas Hardy
Thomas More
Thornton W. Burgess
U. S. Grant
Upton Sinclair
Valentine Williams
Various Authors
Vaughan Kester
Victor Appleton
Victor G. Durham
Victoria Cross
Virginia Woolf
Wadsworth Camp
Walter Camp
Walter Scott
Washington Irving
Wilbur Lawton
Wilkie Collins
Willa Cather
Willard F. Baker
William Dean Howells
William le Queux
W. Makepeace Thackeray
William W. Walter
William Shakespeare
Winston Churchill
Yei Theodora Ozaki
Yogi Ramacharaka
Young E. Allison
Zane Grey

www.ingramcontent.com/pod-product-compliance
Lightning Source LLC
Chambersburg PA
CBHW030330180626
46810CB00003B/1292